# BASIC
# REMODELING
# TECHNIQUES

Created and designed by the
editorial staff of ORTHO Books

Project Editor
Ken Burke

Writer
David Edwards

Designers
Craig Bergquist
Christine Dunham

Illustrator
Ron Hildebrand

# Ortho Books

**Publisher**
Robert L. Iacopi

**Editorial Director**
Min S. Yee

**Managing Editors**
Anne Coolman
Michael D. Smith
Sally W. Smith

**Production Manager**
Ernie S. Tasaki

**Editors**
Jim Beley
Susan Lammers
Deni Stein

**Design Coordinator**
Darcie S. Furlan

**System Managers**
Christopher Banks
Mark Zielinski

**Photographic Director**
Alan Copeland

**Photographers**
Laurie A. Black
Richard A. Christman

**Production Editors**
Linda Bouchard
Alice Mace
Kate O'Keeffe

**Asst. System Manager**
William F. Yusavage

**Chief Copy Editor**
Rebecca Pepper

**Photo Editors**
Anne Dickson-Pederson
Pam Peirce

**National Sales Manager**
Garry P. Wellman

**Sales Associate**
Susan B. Boyle

**Operations Director**
William T. Pletcher

**Operations Assistant**
Gail L. Davis

**Administrative Assistant**
Georgiann Wright

Address all inquiries to
Ortho Books
Chevron Chemical Company
Consumer Products Division
575 Market Street
San Francisco, CA 94105

First Printing in April, 1983

4 5 6 7 8 9

87 88

ISBN 0-89721-016-6

Library of Congress Catalog Card
Number 82-63128

**Chevron Chemical Company**
575 Market Street, San Francisco, CA 94105

## Acknowledgements

**Consulting:**
Robert Beckstrom
Berkeley, CA

Randall Fleming
Oakland, CA

Herb Ziegler
Cambridge, MA

**Photography:**

Front Cover:
Michael Lamotte

Back Cover:
Stephen Marley

Title Page:
David Fischer
Patrick Lyons

Chapter Openings:
Fred Lyon

Styling:
Laura Ferguson
Sara Slavin

**Typography:**
Typothetae
Palo Alto, CA

**Color Separations:**
Colortech
Redwood City, CA

**Additional Illustration:**
Edith Allgood
Brenda Booth
Frank Hildebrand
Bill Oetinger
Jeff Womble

**Illustration Coloring:**
Angela Hildebrand
David Hildebrand
Robyn Hildebrand
Ronda Hildebrand
Marilyn Hill
Carla Simmons

**Copyediting:**
Carol Westberg

**Additional Editing:**
Jessie Wood

**Front Cover Photograph:**
You can tackle many
remodeling jobs with
only a few tools.

**Back Cover Photographs:**
*Upper left* —Sliding glass
doors can bring the outside
into your home.
*Upper right* —A new
skylight allows plants
to thrive indoors.
*Lower left* —The finishing
touches can make a big
difference in cabinets
and counters.
*Lower right* —How you use
available space can make
one room feel like two.

**Title Page Photo:**
Adding a bay window will
give you new views as well
as more light.

# BASIC REMODELING TECHNIQUES

# CONSIDERING THE BASICS

The remodeling you have in mind may change your kitchen cabinets or the tone of your whole house. You should base decisions about what to do and when on careful long-range planning and assessment of the resources at hand.

If you're like most people, the word *remodeling* evokes images of plaster dust, exposed studs, dangling wires, and endless hours of detailed tasks. You're probably seeking information about techniques and procedures for doing such work. Perhaps you feel confident that with proper information you could tackle a project on your own. Or perhaps you intend to hire professionals to do the actual work, but want to know how it's done.

Whatever your situation you'll have dozens of questions buzzing in your head: What is involved? Can I do it? Are my plans and ideas adequate? Where do I begin?

This book is one good place to begin your planning. The text explains about basic structure, materials, and how the work is done. The illustrations demonstrate the techniques used by professional remodelers and experienced do-it-yourselfers.

You'll see by thumbing through this book that it emphasizes practical, step-by-step methods for completing remodeling projects. This is all necessary and useful information, but the most critical and challenging task is the planning that must precede these operations. In fact, the design you work from can easily determine the success or failure of your project. It affects not only the outcome but the work as well. All too often do-it-yourself remodelers (and professionals too) encounter obstacles, setbacks, and surprises that could have been avoided with careful planning.

Planning is much more than a rough sketch on the back of an envelope. Many professionals say that proper planning represents more than a third of the work to be done in any remodeling. You may find that the hardest task ahead isn't toenailing studs in place; it's putting pen to paper and thinking through your project in advance.

But just because it's difficult, don't give planning the

short shrift. As a homeowner you have a tremendous advantage in planning. You have continuous access to your home environment and know the kind of living that goes on there. You can test and revise ideas and change your plans accordingly. You can take your time. And you will have a lot of fun.

Planning, like any other process of remodeling, involves special techniques and procedures. This chapter describes some preliminary work you must do before you start any project.

Chapter 2 will help you to assess the construction of your home—its anatomy—so you can inspect and evaluate it thoroughly. What can be done with the existing house to meet your goals? What should be done first? What can be put off for three or four years? This chapter presents guidelines for the next stage of preparation: bringing your dreams and your plans together.

Chapters 3, 4, and 5 provide specific how-to techniques for getting the work done. If you understand these techniques, you should be able to apply them to whatever situation you encounter.

Finally, the appendix covers other subjects you need to know about such as working with various remodeling professionals, drawing up specifications and materials lists, getting written bids, and working out a contract.

## Establishing Long-Range Goals

If you feel that step one of the planning process is deciding what to do with that awful kitchen or where to add the extra bedroom, you've gone too far. Back up. Your first task, which could take weeks or even months, is to examine your needs, desires, and motivations for wanting to remodel in the first place.

Ask yourself this question: What should our home be like in five years? There is nothing magical about the number five, but it is a realistic time span for accomplishing several remodeling projects in an orderly fashion—projects you might not be able to do all at once because of limited resources. The idea here is not to

Gathering remodeling ideas from photographs, magazines, and library books will help you know your options.

focus on one particular project, even if it solves the most irritating problem at hand. The idea is to see in larger perspective what you and your family really want for your home. Then you can form long-range goals and design projects that best meet those goals.

How does your household discover its wants and needs and set goals? The best way is to make lists. Start a notebook. You'll come back to it time and again. Your initial lists don't have to be well written, logical, or even practical. It is important to include everyone in your family, even future members.

Sit down together and list what you want for your home. Be sure to note your desires as well as your needs, since extravagant fantasies don't cost anything at this stage. There's plenty of time to be practical later. Simply write down what comes to mind. For example:
■ We need more storage
■ Replace the old kitchen cabinets
■ A fireplace
■ Somewhere for the kids to play without being underfoot all the time
■ A feeling of warmth and togetherness
■ A larger dining area
■ A quiet place to study
■ A bright and sunny feeling
■ Secret and private spaces
■ More room for guests
■ An orange wall to go with the blue quilt

Whenever possible, list the underlying reasons for each idea. Why do you want to make the change? Do you need more space, want a more modern look, or intend to make your house more energy-efficient? Reasons are important because they can help bring agreement over differences later on, they can help you see other ways to accomplish the same goals, and they can help you set priorities.

After everyone has had a chance to offer ideas, pool them together. You will have dozens of suggestions and 10, 20, or 50 reasons for them. After some refining and perhaps coming back to the list several times, you will have a tool to be used in the next step, which is to establish a list of concrete goals. These goals may change over the coming weeks and months, but for now read through your first list of ideas carefully. Try to identify the underlying reasons that overlap and build on each other.

These reasons and their suggestions will help generate some specific goals for your home. For example:
■ A kitchen where the family can come together
■ Walk-in closets for clothes
■ A place for formal and elegant entertaining
■ An attractive facade and entry
■ An upstairs master suite
■ A sunny nook for morning coffee
■ A basement rec room for the children

The final step is to rank this list by priorities. What should be done first, second, third, and so on? Again, this list may change over time, but if enough effort has gone into the preparation to this point, your goals should be clear by now.

Many factors contribute to the process of ranking your goals. Urgent needs may cause you to place one goal higher than others. Or you may meet some goals with very little effort and therefore give them high priority. Some goals must be met before others; for instance, new siding should be applied before a deck is added. Some goals may meet the needs of more family members than others. Some may involve more chaos and debris than you're willing to put up with right now. And so on.

Note that no goals are eliminated or compromised —they are merely ranked according to your priorities. This is important. Most likely your budget and time constraints would make a total remodeling or renovation of the house out of the question. Unfortunately, many homeowners still tackle the project all at once and simply squeeze it into the budget by making compromises. They usually end up dissatisfied. It is much easier to see remodeling as an orderly series of steps toward a final goal. You can undertake each step, or project, as time and resources permit. The only compromises are in rearranging priorities, not in reducing the quality of each project.

## Adding to the Value of Your Home

It's likely that underlying all your other reasons for remodeling are financial considerations—improving the value of your home. This may not be a primary motivation, but it shouldn't be overlooked either. Your home represents a tremendous financial investment that should never be neglected.

You need to take care of normal maintenance, of course, but you must also make improvements that keep your home up to date. Items that are considered normal maintenance don't add a great deal to the value of your home. New buyers and appraisers expect a house to be well maintained and may see the new roof or carpeting you've just installed as part of routine care.

Extras such as swimming pools and saunas may not return their full cost either. It's important to keep future buyers in mind when you're planning your remodeling. If you think you may sell your home in the future, think twice about plans that are too unusual or exotic. These changes may actually devalue rather than improve your home's financial worth.

A good remodeling can provide an excellent return on your investment. Real estate appraisers say that certain types of remodelings provide better returns than others. Improvements that bring additional space and utility to a home increase its value most. For example, the addition of a second bathroom or a third bedroom to a two-bedroom house offers a good return on investment. Energy-saving projects such as insulation or solar panels may also prove very attractive to buyers. Of course, since you can't please everyone, you must consider what you value first.

# WHO WILL DO THE WORK

Skilled remodeling professionals are an important resource, one you will want to consider carefully. Early in your planning begin thinking about who will do the actual remodeling work. Is it possible for you to do the work yourself, or would it be best to hire professionals to do it for you? This decision depends on three factors: your personal abilities, the complexity of your plans, and the extent of your budget. You have four basic options:

■ *You hire a designer and a general contractor to handle your entire remodeling.* This means professionals will do all the work for you. Of course you don't just leave town until the job is finished. You are the owner and principal decision maker. You'll need to be available to answer questions and solve problems as they arise. While this option may be the easiest for you, it is also the most expensive.

■ *You hire a general contractor but do some of the work yourself.* Perhaps the contractor will build the shell and close in your new addition; you will finish the interior. Or you may concentrate your efforts in areas that require relatively unskilled labor, such as demolition and site preparation. This is a good option if you have some skills and interest in do-it-yourself work, but neither the time nor the experience to take on much responsibility.

■ *You act as your own general contractor and hire and coordinate the necessary subcontractors.* In this way you save the general contractor's fee, which may be 15 to 20 percent of the job. Acting as your own general contractor requires a lot of organization, time, patience, knowledge of which people to hire, and the ability to deal with them. You may need to provide workers' compensation insurance for the people you employ. Check on this with your insurance agent or the State Compensation Insurance Fund in your area.

■ *You do it all yourself or with nonprofessional help.* You are the designer, the skilled and unskilled laborer, the one who does it all from start to finish. You may find pleasure and satisfaction in the work itself. Or your decision may be based primarily on economics. If you can afford to invest your time, doing all the work yourself can be the least expensive option. And don't overlook the possibility of trading skills with friends or neighbors who have more remodeling experience than you do or who are willing to lend a pair of hands and a strong back to your project. Does your friend need an occasional babysitter so she can spend more time in her carpentry workshop? The American tradition of barn raising is still active in many parts of the country. If you do all of the planning and preparation, the actual work can go quickly and smoothly with volunteer labor. And it's fun besides.

Which option is best for you depends on a number of factors. If you're at all uncertain, it's a good idea to talk to several contractors and designers before you decide. Then you will have a better picture of the skills they offer. Next you should assess your own abilities. Have you thought seriously about how much of the work you can do yourself?

This is no time for false bravado. You need a frank, objective appraisal of your abilities and skills. Otherwise you're only asking for trouble later on. Be realistic. You may be better off hiring professionals to do the job for you. And there's nothing wrong with that. In fact, some codes require electrical and plumbing work, for example, to be done by a licensed professional (see page 93).

But don't sell yourself short because you lack extensive experience. If you have some skills already, this book can supply the how-to instructions you need to complete your project. Perhaps you should handle some small projects first to gain experience and find out if you really enjoy this type of work. You should consider other factors as well when making your decision.

■ *Is the job too technical?* For example, does your remodeling include complicated plumbing and heating installations? Will the work be visible, and does it require skilled craftsmanship? Even though you may know how to do a job, can you do it well? Some skills take years to perfect. If the project requires sophisticated engineering, the services of an architect at the beginning can save you time, trouble, and frustration later.

■ *Does the job require special equipment?* You can buy used tools at garage sales or flea markets. Or you can rent special tools for a weekend or more. But hiring a professional with the right tools may be less expensive than buying new tools that you will never use again.

■ *Is time a factor?* Is there a tight deadline to meet or the threat of bad weather? Can you live with the mess and fatigue that always seem to accompany do-it-yourself projects? Do you have the time to spare? Remodeling projects have been known to drag on for years, when the homeowner can work only on weekends.

■ *Is it worth it economically for you to do the work yourself?* Get out your calculator to figure this. Instead of taking three weeks of vacation and working at home, consider staying at your job and hiring a professional to handle the remodeling. Depending on the size of your project and your salary, you may earn enough in those three weeks to pay for much of it.

Of course no dollar figure can be placed on the satisfaction of tackling a difficult job and completing it successfully. The best way to raise your level of expertise is by hands-on experience. If you start by doing all or most of a small job yourself, just to learn how to do it, you can then move on to a harder task. And if you tackle more than you can handle, you can always call for help. If you get rough estimates from contractors, you may be able to use them to figure how much you can save, or you might wait until you have firm bids. Separate the cost of materials from the labor. Estimate how many hours the job will require for a professional and then multiply in a handicap factor if you do it yourself. For example, if the professional takes ten hours to do the job, multiply this by $1\frac{1}{2}$, 2, or even 3 times for you to do the job. Then figure the hourly rate you'll be paying yourself for doing the work. Is it worth it?

■ *Is the project too strenuous or risky?* Are you physically able to handle the work? Your health is invaluable—don't jeopardize it needlessly.

There are no easy answers here. You're the only one who can assess your particular situation.

# DEVELOPING YOUR PLAN

More than any other factor, planning will make the difference in how your remodeling succeeds. This chapter will help you explore your home's structure, consider your goals, and work out a sound plan.

Before you can begin to make long-range plans, you need to know how your home is put together. This knowledge will help you plan the project better and give you a clear picture of how to proceed.

To a first-time remodeler the anatomy of a house may seem overwhelmingly complex, but actually it's not that complicated or difficult to understand. Standard building procedures vary only slightly throughout the country. Once you've read through the following overview, you'll have a good idea of how most homes are built. You will also be familiar with basic terms for dealing with professionals. Then you should walk through and assess your own home.

Your remodeling plans may progress from doodles, rough sketches, and traffic patterns to working plans.

## The Anatomy of a House

In many ways the structure of your house is like the structure of your body. The skeletal frame provides strength and support. Hidden within the frame are such essentials as electrical, plumbing, and heating systems. The exposed surfaces of the frame and systems are protected by various skins, such as roofing, siding, and wall coverings. Let's inspect the anatomy of a typical house from the ground up. Study the illustrations as you go to visualize how everything fits together.

### The Foundation

Most homes rest on concrete footings that transfer the weight of the house to undisturbed soil beneath the frost line. Above the footings is a foundation wall, which elevates the house above the ground to prevent decay and damage from moisture and insects, especially termites. If your home has no basement or crawl space, the

## A Typical House and Its Foundation

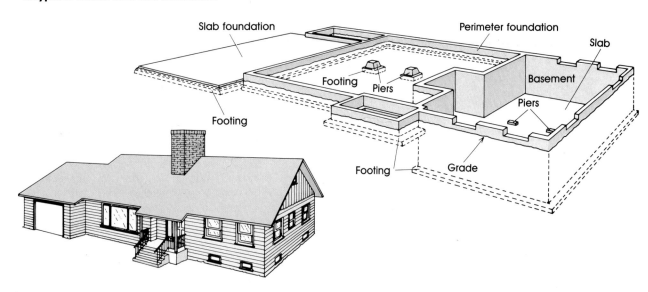

foundation and footings are generally poured together in a single concrete slab.

### The Structural Framework

The wooden framework above the foundation forms the skeleton of your house. Two basic types are used: post-and-beam construction and platform framing. If the type of framing in your house isn't evident from the interior, you will be able to identify it in the attic, basement, or crawl space.

*Post-and-beam construction* was the main type of building until the late nineteenth century, and it's still popular in areas such as New England. Post-and-beam consists of a framework of vertical supports (posts) connected by horizontal spanning members (beams). The wooden timbers are large, perhaps 4 by 12 or 6 by 12 inches. Often the framework is exposed in the interior of the house and easy to identify. Walls between the wooden framework divide the interior space but aren't an essential part of the structural system.

*Platform framing* has been the predominant type of wood construction in the last 80 years or so. A variation called *balloon framing* is common in some older homes. The accompanying illustrations show the differences between balloon and platform framing. Instead of a few massive pieces that support a post-and-beam structure, platform framing employs many smaller pieces of lumber. Each floor is a platform or box that sits on top of the previous floor or platform.

Most homes in the United States today were built with this method, which is the type of construction referred to throughout the rest of this book. Even if the exterior of your home is brick or masonry veneer, the inner structure is probably wood that is platform-framed.

The dimensions of wood used in platform framing have changed over the years. You should keep these slight differences in mind when you plan your re-

### Platform Framing

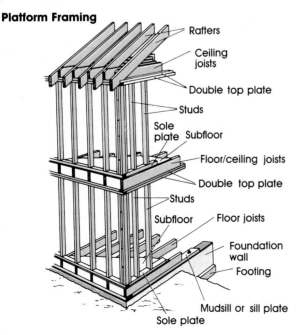

**Post-and-Beam Framing**

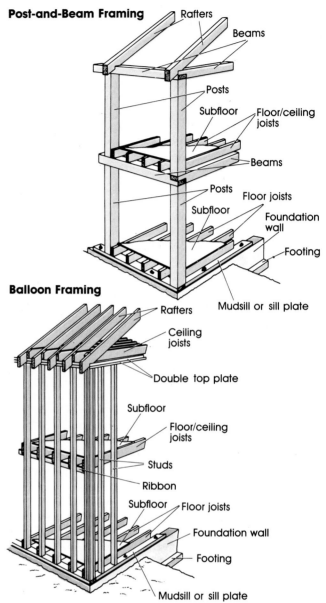

**Balloon Framing**

modeling. If you own an older home, for example the wood may have unplaned surfaces and a rough, almost fuzzy appearance. Those 2 by 4s may measure a full 2 by 4 inches, but in recent years lumber sizes have become smaller (see page 94).

**Floors.** If your home has a slab foundation, the concrete functions as the main platform for the house. If your home has a basement or crawl space, *floor joists* and *subflooring* provide a solid platform for holding up the rest of the house. The joists span the width of the basement and overlap over a main beam called a *girder.* Normal spacing between the joists is 16 inches from center to center, which is often abbreviated *o.c., on center.*

The type of subflooring nailed to the joists depends on the age of your house. If your home was built before 1950, it's likely that boards laid across the joists, either diagonally or perpendicularly, form the subfloor. In post-1950 homes subflooring is either a single layer of plywood or a double system of plywood and hardboard.

## Girders, Floor Joists, and Subflooring

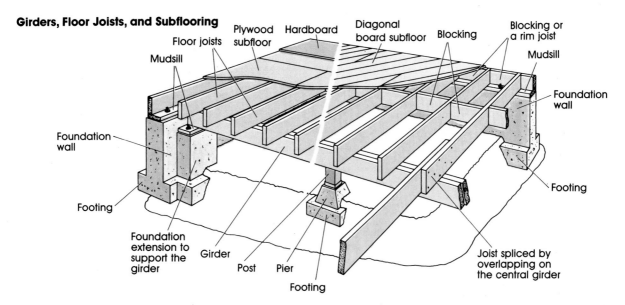

## A Typical Stud Wall

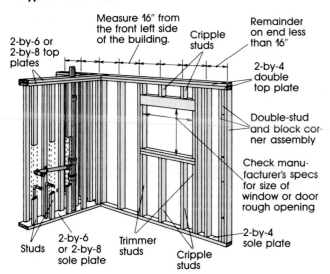

**Walls.** Both the exterior and interior walls of your home are framed with vertical studs nailed 16 inches on center between a bottom plate and two upper plates made from 2 by 4s. The framing is normally 2-by-4 lumber, but there are exceptions. For example, the first floor of a three-story house and newer homes built in cold climates may have 2-by-6 exterior walls. Also, the framing of one wall in your bathroom, called a *wet wall*, may be wider than 2 by 4 to accommodate large drain pipes.

A word of caution: you may find odd spacing between the studs in your home. Don't assume conventional spacing until you've actually checked the walls you're going to work on.

All exterior walls and some interior walls in your house are *bearing walls*. This means they are a principal support for the weight of the roof and floors above them. A bearing wall transfers its load to the ground through the foundation or through a girder and posts. The *nonbearing* or *partition walls* in your house do little

but divide the interior space. They support only the weight of the materials nailed to their surfaces.

In general, nonbearing walls can be easily removed without affecting the structural stability of your house. Bearing walls cannot. To remove a bearing wall you must provide a permanent alternative means of support, such as a beam and posts. (For more information on how to identify and remove bearing and nonbearing walls, see pages 30 and 41.)

**Ceilings.** The ceiling joists in your home provide a nailing surface for the finish ceiling and add stability to the framing by tying the exterior walls together. If your home has two stories or more, the ceiling joists for the lower levels are also the floor joists for the upper level. The framing procedure is simply repeated to complete another story, or platform. Once the top floor is reached, roof rafters are nailed in place, and the structural framework of the house is complete.

### Exterior Surfaces

The exterior surfaces of your house add stability to the structure and form a protective skin that covers the framework. It's not necessary at this point to go into specific detail about how each material is applied. For now visualize your home's roofing as three layers: wood sheathing or decking nailed to the rafters; building paper; and a finishing roofing material such as shingles, shakes, tiles, or tar and gravel. In some cases the local building code determines which roofing finishes you can use.

The exterior walls of your house can be summarized in a similar way: wood sheathing nailed to the outside of the studs, followed by a layer of building paper, and finally a finish siding material, such as wood, vinyl, aluminum, stucco, or brick veneer.

### Interior Walls and Ceilings

Depending on the climate and the age of your house, the cavity between the exterior sheathing and interior wall surface may be filled with insulation. Fiberglass batts or blown-in loose fill are commonly used.

### Three-Layer Roofing System

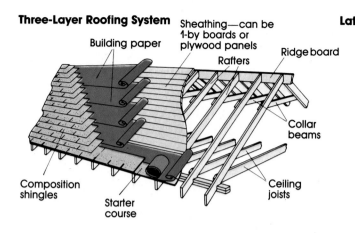

Building paper
Sheathing—can be 1-by boards or plywood panels
Ridge board
Rafters
Collar beams
Ceiling joists
Composition shingles
Starter course

### Lath and Plaster Surfaces

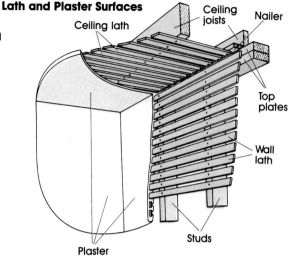

Ceiling lath
Ceiling joists
Nailer
Top plates
Wall lath
Studs
Plaster

### Exterior Wall Covering

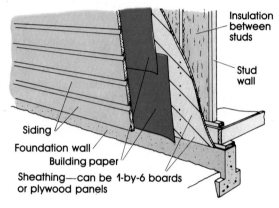

Insulation between studs
Stud wall
Siding
Foundation wall
Building paper
Sheathing—can be 1-by-6 boards or plywood panels

### Wallboard Surfaces

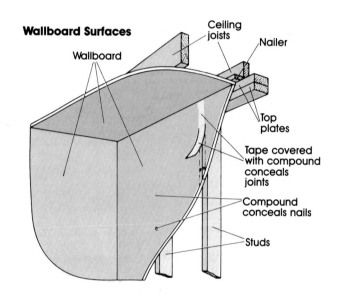

Ceiling joists
Nailer
Wallboard
Top plates
Tape covered with compound conceals joints
Compound conceals nails
Studs

Most interior walls and ceilings in your home are covered with one of three materials: lath and plaster, wallboard, or wood paneling. If your home was built before 1950, the walls and ceilings are probably *lath and plaster.* Lath is thin strips of wood nailed directly to the studs and ceiling joists, over which several coats of plaster are applied.

If your home was built after 1950, the walls and ceilings are probably panels of *wallboard*, a sandwich of ½-inch gypsum between two layers of heavy paper. Wallboard is also called drywall, gypsumboard, or Sheetrock, which is a trade name. The type of wallboard finish depends on the function and decor of the room. Your house may have some wallboard surfaces that are painted or wallpapered, while others are first covered with a skim coat of plaster and then finished.

*Wood paneling* can be individual boards or large panels. If your home has boards applied in a horizontal pattern, they are probably nailed directly to the studs. If the boards are applied vertically, a system of wood strips called *furring* is nailed to the studs first to provide a nailing surface for the boards.

If the paneling is applied in 4- by 8-foot sheets, it's made of plywood. Thin panels nailed directly to the studs tend to ripple and have a hollow sound. The usual method of application is to nail wallboard to the studs and then nail and glue on the paneling. The interior wall covering completes the basic structure of the house.

### Wood Surfaces

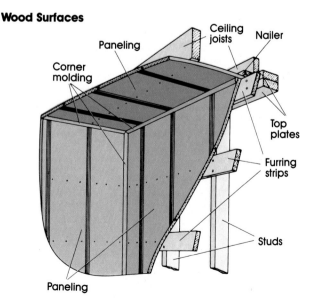

Ceiling joists
Nailer
Paneling
Corner molding
Top plates
Furring strips
Studs
Paneling

## Mechanical Systems

Intertwined within the structural framework of your house are three essential systems: electrical, plumbing, and heating. Even if you don't plan to work with these systems directly, it's difficult to do much remodeling without exposing them somewhat.

**The electrical system.** The electrical system in your house consists of a *service entrance*, where power enters the house, and various *circuits* composed of wires, outlets, and fixtures that distribute the power throughout the house. Safeguards are built into the system to prevent shocks, overheating of wires, and short circuits between wires that shouldn't be touching each other. The *main disconnect*, a switching device that can shut off all power in the house, may be a pull lever, a fuse block that is pulled out, or a main circuit breaker that can be flipped off. It may be housed in a panel box of its own, but it is often in the same panel as the fuses or circuit breakers for all the house circuits.

The main fuse block or circuit breaker has a limit to the electrical load it can carry. If that limit is exceeded, the breaker will automatically shut off electricity to the entire house, which prevents the entrance wires from overheating and causing a fire. This maximum current is called the *service rating*. Most homes today are wired for 100-, 150-, or 200-ampere service. However, older homes without updated wiring may have only 60- or even 30-amp service. The rating is determined by the size of the service-entrance wires and cannot be increased unless they are replaced with larger wires.

Once power enters the house through the service entrance, it is distributed through the circuits originating in the service panel. You may have from 4 to 20 separate circuits in your house, each protected by its own fuse or circuit breaker located in the panel. When a particular circuit is overloaded, the fuse or breaker shuts off power to that circuit and prevents its wires from overheating. You should know which circuits serve each room in your house. Since this circuit wiring is concealed, you may never see it unless you crawl into the attic, open up a wall, or need to wire additional outlets and fixtures.

The service panel itself must be properly grounded by connecting it with a No. 6 wire to a metal water pipe, a copper-clad rod driven deep into the ground, an exposed end of foundation rebar, or a combination of the three. In turn, each outlet and fixture should be attached to a ground wire that leads back to the service-panel ground. When a short circuit or other malfunction occurs, the resulting surge of electrical power flows harmlessly through the grounding wire and to the ground, which is at zero volts. The surge also causes the fuse or circuit breaker to trip, shutting off the affected circuit.

In addition to proper grounding, *ground fault circuit interrupters* (GFCIs) are now required in all bathroom, garage, and outdoor receptacles. These devices prevent a person's body from becoming a grounding path should a malfunction occur while handling equipment plugged into the receptacle.

For a more complete discussion of how to do your own wiring, see Ortho's book *Basic Wiring Techniques*.

## Service Panels

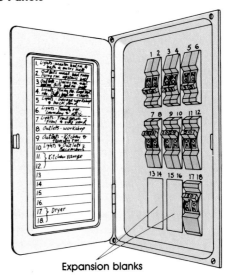

Expansion blanks

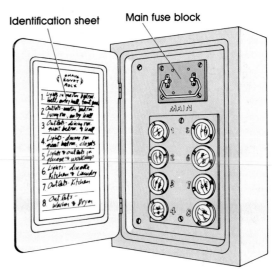

Identification sheet    Main fuse block

## Meter and Service Entrances

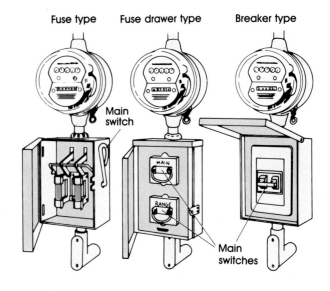

Fuse type    Fuse drawer type    Breaker type

Main switch

Main switches

**The plumbing system.** Besides the actual fixtures, the plumbing in your home consists of two basic systems: a water supply system and a drain-waste-vent (DWV) system. The supply system provides water under pressure; the DWV system carries away water and wastes by gravity, and gases by convection.

■ *Water supply lines.* A *main* or *service line* supplies your home with cold, fresh water. The main normally comes through a basement wall or lower-level utility area. If your home is connected to a municipal water system, the water enters under pressure and travels through a meter. In private supply systems, water is pumped from a well or cistern into a holding tank. Air pressure in the tank creates sufficient water pressure for household use.

Once inside the house the main water line splits into smaller branch lines. One of these goes directly to your water heater. From there hot-water branch lines travel to fixtures that demand hot water, such as the kitchen sink and the bathroom washbasin, tub, and shower.

Cold-water supply lines also split from the main into different branches. One branch, for example, may supply water to the kitchen sink, another may supply water to an upstairs bathroom, and a third branch may supply an outdoor sprinkler system.

*Shutoff valves,* an essential part of your water supply system, are very helpful in remodeling. A main shutoff valve, located where the main line enters the house, will turn off the water to the entire house. Each branch run should also have a shutoff valve, as well as the inlet line to the water heater. Fixture supply valves beneath washbasins and toilets allow you to turn off the water to a particular fixture whenever necessary.

■ *The DWV system.* The drain-waste-vent system depends on gravity to carry wastes away, which means the direction and pitch of the pipes is critical. A drain pipe must slope downward 1/4 inch for every foot of horizontal run—otherwise water would stand in the pipes and sludge would build up.

## Drain-Waste-Vent and Water Supply Systems

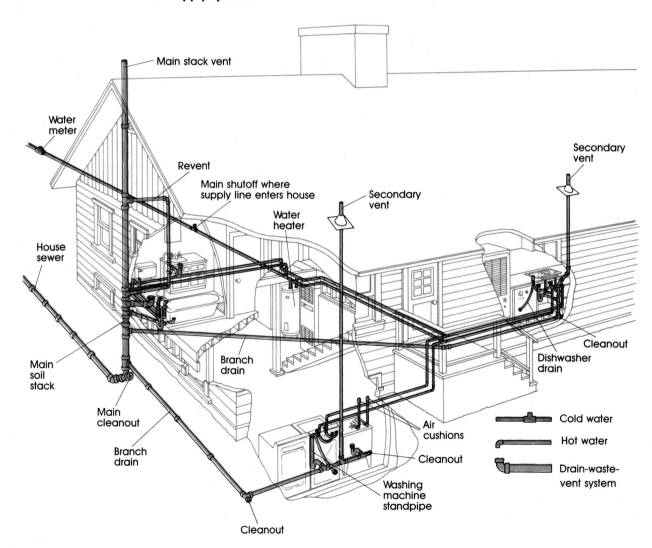

Each fixture or drain in the house must have a *trap* beneath it, a U-shaped dip in the line that remains filled with water. The trap seals off the waste line and prevents noxious fumes as well as vermin from entering the house.

*Cleanout fittings* allow access to each drain in case of plugging. Drain lines from each trap carry the wastes to a vertical pipe called a *soil stack*. The stack connects to the main house drain, which empties into a private septic tank or municipal sewage system.

*Vent pipes* are an integral part of the DWV system. These pipes rise vertically from the drain lines and connect to one or more vent stacks that exit through the roof of the house. The vents bring fresh air into the waste system and carry away unpleasant or dangerous gases that may accumulate.

Both the supply and DWV lines run within the walls and floors of the house. Holes are simply drilled through studs, joists, and plates wherever the pipes need to run. Code limitations on the size of notches and holes prevent the structural strength of the framework from being weakened. In some instances cuts in the studs and joists must be reinforced with metal plates to protect the integrity of the framing.

■ *Gas lines.* Your remodeling project may involve altering gas lines. Although some homeowners are able to do this work themselves, with proper permits, you will probably need professional help. Among other things, gas lines must be sized carefully to ensure a steady flow of gas under pressure to the farthest fixtures. Also, only certain kinds of pipe, fittings, and joint compounds are allowed for gas lines.

■ *Septic systems.* For some remodelers, adding a bathroom or building a room addition may mean enlarging a septic system or even relocating it. This will involve installing a septic tank of the correct size, providing a vent (if needed), and laying an adequate array of leach lines. You should be familiar with the type and age of your system.

For more information about plumbing projects, see Ortho's book *Basic Plumbing Techniques.*

**The heating system.** Unlike electrical and plumbing systems, which are essentially the same everywhere, heating systems vary widely in the type of energy they use and the means of distributing it. Some homes rely on space heaters—woodstoves, fireplaces, portable heaters, or wall or floor heaters. More commonly one of four types of central heating systems is in use, with solar alternatives becoming more prevalent in certain areas.

■ *Forced air.* This is the most common central heating system. The heat producer is a furnace that burns oil, gas, wood, or coal inside a combustion chamber. Waste gases are vented outside through a metal flue and masonry chimney. When the air surrounding the combustion chamber gets hot, it's distributed through the house in a network of ducts. In a slab foundation the ductwork is generally embedded in the concrete. With a crawl space or full basement, sheet metal ducts run underneath and between the floor joists. In a two-story house the upper-level ducts run up the walls, hidden between studs or inside closets.

The furnace is turned on and off automatically by a thermostat, but the heat supply to each room can also be controlled manually. Dampers inside the ducts and at each register open and close to regulate the incoming warm air.

■ *Hot water.* In a hot-water (also called hydronic) system, the furnace is a boiler fueled by oil, gas, electricity, or coal. The boiler heats water to about 200°F, and small pipes (½ to 1 inch) made of galvanized steel or copper distribute the hot water to each room of the house.

If steam and cast-iron radiators are used, the system works with gravity. Pressure from the boiler and lighter density cause the steam to rise naturally within the pipes. Once it circulates through the radiator and condenses, the cooled water returns via the same pipe to the boiler, where the cycle begins again.

In a modern hot-water system, water is forced through the pipes by a circulating pump. Like a plumbing system, the hydronic system has a main supply line that branches from the boiler into two or more supply runs, or zones. After serving each room, the cooled water is cycled back to the boiler by a return line. Separate temperature controls are provided in different parts of the house.

The heat is dissipated into the room by baseboard heaters, which fit unobtrusively along the floor, most often along the outside wall of the house. Generally they're only 8 to 10 inches high and 2 to 3 inches deep.

■ *Electric radiant.* Homes equipped with electric radiant heat have no furnace, ducts, flue, or chimney. The source

| Central Heating Systems | | | |
|---|---|---|---|
| **System** | **Heat Source** | **How Distributed** | **Comments** |
| **Forced Air** | Gas, oil, coal, wood | Ducts, vents, and registers | Relatively economical; easy to add air conditioning, humidifiers, air cleaners; drafty and noisy |
| **Hot Water** | Gas, oil, coal, electricity | Pipes, radiators, baseboard heaters | Even supply of heat; efficient energy conversion; slow to heat up |
| **Electric Radiant** | Electricity | Wires in walls and floors; radiant panels | Comfortable; efficient energy conversion; expensive to operate |
| **Heat Pump** | Electricity, atmosphere, or earth | Ducts, vents | Works best in mild climate; needs electric backup system |
| **Solar** | Sunlight | Ducts, convective air currents | Adds new living space; free heat; must be carefully engineered; requires major construction; needs backup system |

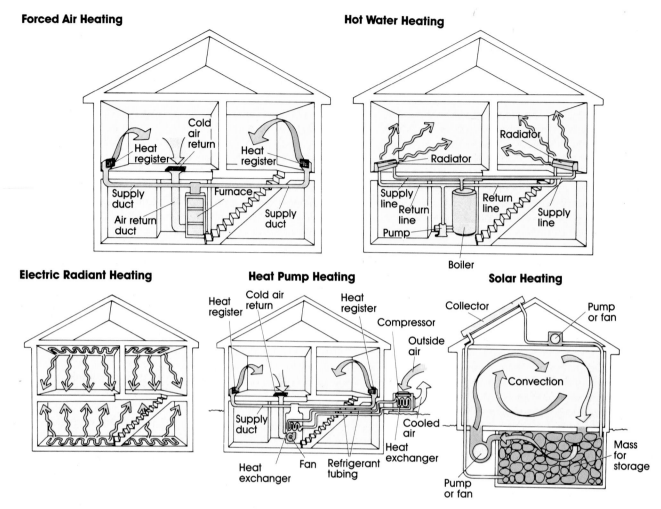

**Forced Air Heating**

**Hot Water Heating**

**Electric Radiant Heating**

**Heat Pump Heating**

**Solar Heating**

of heat is electricity flowing through resistance wiring, which can be installed in the ceiling between two layers of wallboard or beneath the plaster.

In mild climates the wiring is often located in the floor, embedded in the concrete slab. If the wiring is not in the floor or ceiling, baseboard panels are mounted along the floor. Some electric baseboards use only resistance wiring to heat the room. Others use electricity to heat water permanently sealed in copper tubing. Each heater is a self-contained hydronic system that needs no plumbing or separate water supply. Air drawn from the floor passes over the fins of the tubing and circulates upward to warm the room. The hot water continues to provide heat after the electricity is turned off by a thermostat.

■ *Heat pump.* The heat pump is a combination heating and cooling system that operates like a central air conditioner, with a reverse cycle for heating. Electricity is the energy source. In the summer the system withdraws heat from inside the house and dispels it outdoors. In the winter it extracts heat from the outside air and pumps it inside. The air is distributed through the house via sheet-metal ducts just like a forced-air system. If the temperature drops below a certain level, auxiliary electric resistance heaters kick in to provide supplementary heat.

■ *Solar.* Until recently heating systems were usually chosen on the basis of output of BTUs, fuel cost, and convenience of installation. Skyrocketing energy costs have caused homeowners, builders, and architects to consider heating systems from the standpoint of energy efficiency as well. Furthermore, they are not only concerned with how efficiently the heat is produced, but with how well the home retains it. Conservation measures like insulation, weatherstripping, and caulking are at least as important as installing an adequate heating system.

The most efficient and innovative designs are now tapping direct sunlight as the major heat contributor. The means of collecting it can be as simple as increasing the number of south-facing windows or attaching a hot-air collector to a south wall. Or it can be as complex as a complete redesign of the home to incorporate additional south glazing, substantial amounts of heavy mass, and a floor design that creates an optimum flow of natural air currents. In all cases solar heating designs require a home site with continuous exposure to the sun during the cold winter months for at least the four hours from 10 a.m. to 2 p.m.

For more information on assessing energy efficiency along with your other home needs, see Ortho's book *Energy-Saving Projects for the Home.*

# ASSESSING YOUR HOME

Now it's time to take a close look at the actual construction and condition of your home. This is important to do before any remodeling for two reasons: you may discover problems that need attention, and you will find it easier to plan remodeling projects that are compatible with the existing structure.

How thorough does your assessment need to be? That depends. If your plans are simple and confined to a specific part of your house, your survey can be localized. Whenever you need more living space or additional plumbing or wiring, however, make a complete survey. An in-depth assessment is invaluable in making long-range plans for your home.

## Examining Structure and Site

Besides inspecting the construction and condition of the structure, you will be noting your home's use of space; the potential of the site for expansion, views, and solar exposure; and existing features that can make your home more livable.

The actual inspection involves a systematic survey of your entire house—inside, outside, under, and above. You can do it yourself or hire a professional. If you are having an architect do design work, he or she will most likely begin with a thorough house inspection. For projects such as enlarging rooms or adding a second story, it's definitely wise to have a professional help with your survey. For a list of the skills and responsibilities of different remodeling professionals, see page 93.

If you do your own inspection, you will first need to draw up rough floor plan sketches of each room in your house plus the attic and basement or crawl space. Make them large enough to record essential dimensions and fixtures. You can keep these sketches in your project notebook.

Use the survey checklist on the next page as a guide, adding notes of your own and ignoring parts that do not apply to your home. Keep the following tips in mind:

■ Do the survey with a member of your household. It's easier, and one of you is bound to notice things the other may overlook. It's also more fun.

■ Wear comfortable, long-sleeved, old clothes that allow you to crawl in tight or dirty spaces.

■ Carry the following tools: flashlight, screwdriver or ice pick, tape measure (16 feet or longer), small level or marble, clipboard with pad and floor plan, and pencils.

■ Follow this sequence, as much as possible: inspect all interior rooms, the crawl space or basement, exterior areas, the roof, and finally the attic.

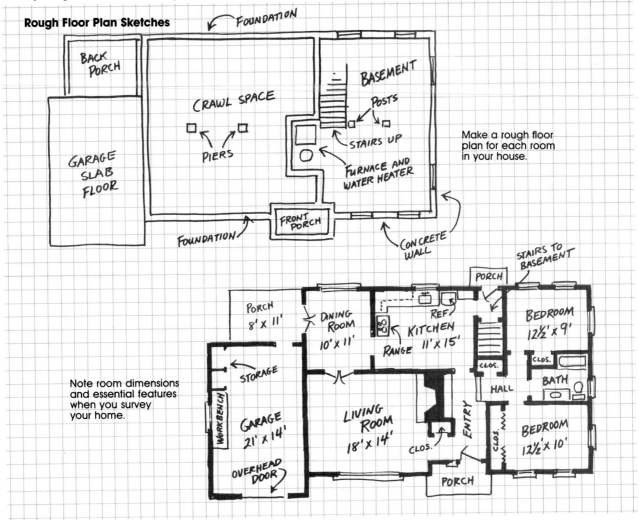

**Rough Floor Plan Sketches**

Make a rough floor plan for each room in your house.

Note room dimensions and essential features when you survey your home.

### Examining Circulation

Once you have surveyed your home inside and out, it's time to assess another important aspect—how you use the space. What is an excellent room layout for one family may not be for another. You need to consider not only your household's activities but also how activity in one location will affect people in another.

In planning your remodeling, you can apply specific rules of circulation and room layout. You should become familiar with certain planning guidelines and key dimensions whether you hire a professional or plan your project yourself.

The interior layout of your home is based on the relationships among three principal areas. *The living or public area* includes the living room, family room, dining area, and any outdoor decks or patios used for entertaining. *The sleeping or private area* includes the bedrooms and private baths. *The working or utility area* is the kitchen, main bathroom, laundry, and service areas. Traffic patterns and hallways connect these areas and allow passage between them. Several factors determine the best ways to arrange these areas.

■ The need to separate noisy areas from quiet areas
■ The use of buffers, such as closets, utility areas, hallways, and stairways
■ The outside environment, including views, parking, sunlight, wind, and external noise
■ The existing structure—its limitations and possibilities
■ Access to other rooms
■ Arrangements in other homes, inns, or ideas books that please you
■ Your underlying reasons for remodeling (Your initial goal may have been to add a family room, but the reason may really be to bring members of the household together more.)
■ Circulation patterns

Traffic flow and circulation are a major consideration in room layouts. Although areas must be separated, they need to be properly related as well. Circulation provides the key to a good floor plan. Keep these considerations in mind as you lay out your remodeling.

■ *Smooth and efficient circulation.* Keep hallways and traffic areas to a minimum, but avoid creating disruptions or bottlenecks.

### A Survey Checklist

As you survey your house, record dimensions and mechanical system and fixture locations on your floor plan sketches. Keep notes on construction, condition, and design considerations on a separate sheet for each room or area.

#### Interior Rooms
#### Construction and condition
■ Length, width, and height of room
■ Door, closet, and window dimensions
■ Type of finish floor, layers, slope (check with marble or level), stability (check for bounce or squeaks), damage
■ Finish wall and ceiling materials, damage
■ Door and window materials and condition

#### Fixtures and mechanical systems
■ Built-ins such as cabinets, fireplace, shelves
■ Major furnishings and appliances
■ Electrical outlets, switches, lights, and circuits
■ Plumbing fixtures, pipes, and shutoff valves
■ Heating registers or radiators
■ Gas pipes, ducts, flues

#### Design aspects
■ Views, sources of light, eyesores
■ Noise, distractions from outside
■ Use of space
■ Overall feeling (open, crowded, active, dark, intimate, etc.)
■ Special features

#### Room-by-room considerations
■ Kitchen—counter space, condition of cabinets, condition of sink
■ Bedrooms—window for emergency exit, walls with no window
■ Bathrooms—ventilation, sealing around tub, condition of toilet and washbasin
■ Hallways—lighting, potential entrances
■ Stairs—lighting; safety of risers, treads, rails

#### Crawl Space or Basement
#### Construction and condition
■ Length, width, and height
■ Door, stairway, window dimensions
■ Location and size of girders and posts
■ Direction, size, span, and spacing of joists (are they level?)
■ Size and spacing of cripple studs
■ Type and condition of foundation (all wood 8 inches above grade?)
■ Size and depth of footing
■ Condition of sills
■ Location of anchor bolts
■ Material and condition of floor (evidence of seepage or leakage, especially under bathrooms and kitchen)
■ Insulating material and condition
■ Termite tubes, wood debris, or weak structural wood

#### Fixtures and mechanical systems
■ Major utilities (furnace, sump pump)
■ Location of main drain and water supply
■ Condition of pipes and ducts
(problems with support, corrosion, rust, clearance, or cleanouts)

#### Design aspects
■ Current and potential access and sources of light
■ Potential for living space
■ New posts or bearing walls needed for upstairs remodeling

■ *Entries and exits.* The front door should be relatively close to the driveway or street. It should open into an entry area that provides smooth access to the main living areas and blocks views into the private areas. If possible, there should be a secondary entrance from the garage or driveway to the kitchen. In colder climates consider an air-lock entry for more efficient heating.

■ *Room-to-room circulation.* No plan should have a box-car arrangement of rooms in which access to one room is always through another. In particular the living room and kitchen should be protected from too much through traffic.

■ *Within-room circulation.* The layout of each room should allow free passage through the room and around furniture. Ideally, no room should have so many doorways that only one furniture arrangement is possible. Generally it's better to locate a door close to an adjacent wall rather than in the middle of the wall.

■ *Hallways and entryways.* There should be sufficient room for moving furniture. The minimum acceptable width is 3 feet, but 3 feet 6 inches is better. Stairs and landings also must be wide enough for moving furniture.

## Room-by-Room Planning

Your completed house inspection should provide new data for revising and refining your goals. Perhaps it revealed urgent problems that should get priority attention, or even require demolition and replacement. Look at such situations as opportunities for redesigning your home rather than as unexpected headaches. If your home has no problems, at least you're more aware of its construction and all the features you want to preserve.

The next step is design. Design is probably the single most important aspect of your remodeling, so important that it can easily determine the success or failure of your project. Many people associate the word *design* with style and decoration. But in the context of planning a home, it means much more. It means an overall plan that offers the best solution to problems presented by the situation at hand. Design decisions involve intangibles. Often there is no one right answer. Any problem may have a number of good workable solutions.

In planning individual rooms, common sense often determines the appropriateness of space and furniture arrangement. Your experience and house inspection

---

■ Furnace, pipes, or other obstructions
■ Possible problems (seepage, headroom, heating, drains, uneven floor)

### Exterior Areas
#### Construction and condition
■ Type and condition of siding (wood within 8 inches of ground?)
■ Condition of doors, windows, and frames
■ Condition of steps, handrails, and walkways
■ Cracks, chips, or lean of chimney
■ Plates or leaders on downspouts
■ Condition of deck (number and strength of footings, span for girder and stringer, spacing for joists, metal brackets, loose or rotted boards)

#### Site and landscaping
■ Lot dimensions and location of house and garage
■ Existing and potential parking areas
■ Direction of slope; evidence of soil movement
■ Direction of rising, noon, and setting sun
■ Direction of views, eyesores, nearby houses
■ Existing and potential garden areas and trees
■ Nearby storm drains
■ Location of water meter, gas meter or LP gas tank, septic tank and leach lines, sewer lines

#### Design aspects
■ Overall size, scale, and proportion of house
■ Potential for expansion (zoning or setback laws)
■ Appealing and unappealing aspects of house
■ Serious and minor structural and maintenance problems

### Roof
#### Construction and condition
■ Dimensions, slope, valleys, hips

■ Location and condition of skylights, hatches, chimneys, flues, and vents
■ Type, layer, and condition of roofing material (patches, leakage, rot)
■ Condition of gutters, decking

#### Design aspects
■ Significant views
■ Potential or existing rooftop deck areas
■ Access

### Attic
#### Construction and condition
■ Size and spacing of joists and rafters
■ Height of ridge line and collar beams
■ Location, dimensions of door, stairway, windows
■ Permanent subfloor
■ Chimney, flues, vents, and exhaust outlets
■ Adequate ventilation
■ Insulation in ceiling, rafters, ducts
■ Signs of leakage
■ Location and condition of light fixtures, outlets, wiring

#### Design aspects
■ Potential for storage and living space
■ Access
■ Potential for dormers or openings to rooms below

### Electrical System Details
■ Number of wires entering service head
■ Location of service and branch panels
■ Service rating of main disconnect
■ Location of circuits and corresponding fuses or breakers
■ Condition of wiring
■ Service panel and outlet grounding

notes will guide you in many instances. But here are some overall considerations to remember.

■ *Consider key activity centers.* Some rooms serve a single function only; others may have several uses. Imagine how your household members might use each room—for conversation, reading, game playing, television viewing, sleeping, and so forth. Also consider where guests tend to gather.

■ *What is the physical space like?* Is the room large enough? Is it too large? If so, there may be visual and auditory problems. What is the shape of the room? Are the proportions pleasant? In general it's best to keep room shapes simple for effective use of space and low construction costs.

■ *How can you affect living quality?* Does the room offer more than function? Its size, shape, placement and size of windows and doors all contribute to the overall feeling. Are the views distracting? Is the light appropriate? Does the space suggest activity, rest, or interaction?

■ *Don't overlook details.* Minor details can make a big difference in how a room works. For example, do the doors swing the right way? Do they cause awkward disruptions? You may have enough light switches and electrical outlets, but are they accessible? Are closet space and storage adequate? Are several furniture arrangements possible?

■ *Do you have enough light and ventilation?* Would a skylight or more windows help? Is the artificial lighting adequate? Even if you have air conditioning, each room should have natural ventilation as well.

■ *Can you improve energy efficiency?* Do windows face south for heat gain in colder areas? Is shading from trees available? Do ceiling height and expansive window areas affect heat loss?

As you go room by room developing your plans, take your floor plan sketches along. One good way to play with alternative room arrangements is to make templates on graph paper like the ones in the illustrations. They needn't be exactly to scale, but the walls, fixtures, built-ins, and furniture should be reasonably proportional.

## Kitchens

First, consider the overall purpose of your kitchen. Is it to be a work center only? Or a multipurpose room for dining and family activities? Second, decide which type of eating arrangement you prefer. Do you want a breakfast nook, a serving counter, an alcove that's part of the kitchen or living room, or a completely separate dining room? Third, arrange the various activity centers to provide the most efficient kitchen plan.

Every kitchen has three main activity centers.

■ The food storage center includes the refrigerator/freezer, cabinets, and counter space.

■ The cleanup center includes the sink, counter space on either side, a garbage disposer, a dishwasher, and trash compactor.

■ The cooking center includes a range or cooktop, oven, counter space on either side, ventilating equipment, and cabinets and drawers for utensils.

The efficient arrangement of these three centers is called a *work triangle.* At least five good layouts are common.

■ The *U-shaped kitchen* is generally considered the most desirable. It offers continuous counter area and the shortest walking distance between appliances.

■ The *corridor kitchen* is the simplest and often the most economical arrangement. The corridor should be at least four feet wide to allow traffic to pass, but the kitchen location should not encourage through traffic.

## Types of Kitchen Layouts

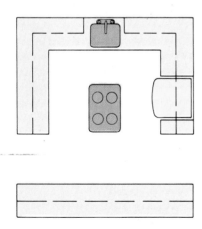

Island U-shaped kitchen

Island L-shaped kitchen

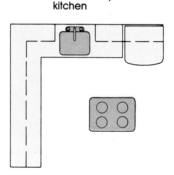

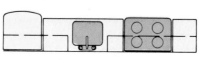

One-wall kitchen

Corridor kitchen

■ The *L-shaped kitchen* creates an eating area adjacent to the work triangle and eliminates through traffic.

■ The *island kitchen*, a modified U- or L-shape, is a good plan for two people who like to cook together. If you use the island as the cooking center, venting can be a problem.

■ The *one-wall kitchen* is the least desirable layout, but may be necessary in some situations. If it is, the sink should be in the center of the work flow. The overall length of the kitchen wall should be no more than 13 feet.

The location of each activity center determines the efficiency of the kitchen. For example, the range should not be located next to the refrigerator. Nor should the range be located directly under a window. Breezes may interfere with gas burners, and curtains can catch fire. The local code may determine the location of the range for venting and safety, so check on this. The sink is best located under a window for natural light and a view. The dishwasher should be within 12 inches of the sink but not so its door blocks traffic.

Keep the following dimensions in mind.

■ Recommended distances for the three sides of the work triangle are: 4 to 7 feet from the sink to the refrigerator, 4 to 6 feet from the sink to the range, and 4 to 9 feet from the range to the refrigerator. This means that no two basic appliances should be less than 4 feet apart.

■ The total perimeter of the work triangle should be 12 to 22 feet.

■ For efficiency the overall size of the kitchen should be not more than 160 square feet.

■ Allow 15 to 18 inches of counter space on the latch side of the refrigerator for loading and unloading.

■ Allow 30 to 36 inches of counter space on both sides of the sink.

■ Allow at least 24 inches of counter space on both sides of the range; 30 inches is preferable.

■ Countertops are normally 24 inches deep and 32 to 36 inches high, depending on personal preference and comfort.

■ For specific appliance and cabinet sizes, measure your existing units carefully or take new dimensions from manufacturers' catalogs and data sheets. Be sure to allow sufficient space for doors to swing open completely.

For more information and ideas about kitchen planning, see Ortho's book *How to Design and Remodel Kitchens.*

## Bathrooms

First, consider the overall function of the bath. Is it a half-bath with a washbasin and toilet, or is it a full family bath? Do you want to include a dressing area or laundry equipment? What about extras such as a sauna or steam bath? Will the bath be used by all family members or only a few? The main family bathroom should be located so that it is easily accessible from all bedrooms.

Economy is an important consideration in deciding on locations and layout. Use existing plumbing lines whenever possible to save on labor and material costs. This means a back-to-back arrangement with another

bath or kitchen, or an upstairs bath located over the first-floor plumbing connections.

The layout of the principal fixtures can be a U-shaped, L-shaped, or corridor arrangement. If you live in a cold climate, locate the water supply and drain-waste-vent lines in an interior wall to prevent freezing. Avoid a layout that allows a door to swing into any fixture. Don't locate the tub under a window. Cold drafts can be uncomfortable, and the window is more difficult to open with the tub in the way. The best tub layout is enclosed by three walls or an alcove.

Several dimensions are specified by the plumbing code (check your local code for additional spacing).

■ Generally a full bathroom requires a space at least 5 by 7 feet.

■ The thickness of the wet wall that conceals the drains and soil stack may need to be 2 by 6 inches rather than 2 by 4.

■ Allow a minimum of 24 inches from the front rim of a toilet to a facing wall.

■ Allow 18 inches from the center line of the toilet to an adjacent wall and 15 inches to an adjacent fixture.

■ The minimum size for a shower stall is 32 by 32 inches.

For specific fixture sizes, measure the existing fixtures carefully or take new dimensions from manufacturers' catalogs and data sheets. For more information and ideas on planning a bathroom, see Ortho's book *How to Design and Remodel Bathrooms.*

**Bathroom Layouts and Clearances**

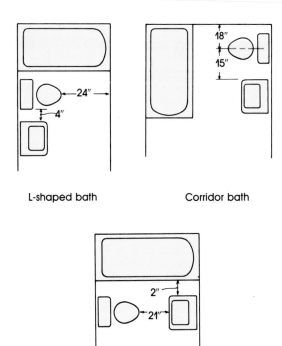

L-shaped bath          Corridor bath

U-shaped bath

## Living Room Layouts and Traffic Patterns

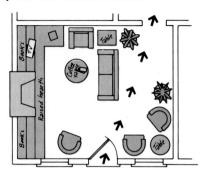

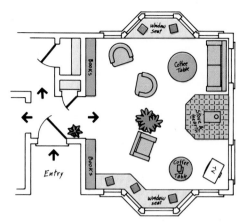

### Living Rooms

The typical living room must serve several functions with a single furniture arrangement. First, list all the activities that will be going on in the room. Then select furnishings to fit those activities. This works better than creating a room scheme around a particular piece of furniture.

Plan your furniture arrangement for maximum flexibility. You'll need to have access to several activity areas at the same time. Avoid plans that require rearranging furniture every time you want to play a game or watch TV.

Create one primary conversation grouping around a main focal point, such as a fireplace or picture window. Through traffic in this area should be kept to a minimum. If you have a large family or enjoy entertaining, allow seating for at least eight people in this primary furniture grouping. Arrange the seating so that conversation can take place without anyone twisting uncomfortably in his or her seat.

Depending on your family's needs and interests, you may also want to provide secondary furniture groupings for reading, writing, listening to music and playing musical instruments, game playing, and TV viewing. Plan for TV viewers to be seated at no more than a 45-degree angle from the set. Keep in mind that viewing becomes difficult beyond 10 or 12 feet.

Traffic patterns are critical. The number of entry/exits to the living room should be kept to a minimum. An entrance hall or foyer should provide direct access to other rooms of the house, thereby protecting the living room.

The following dimensions will affect your planning.
■ Although it's difficult to give a minimum size, 12 by 18 feet is considered a small to modest size for a living room.
■ The maximum distance that allows a comfortable arc of conversation is between 6 and 8 feet.
■ The minimum width for general traffic is 40 inches. If there is only one doorway to the living area, increase this traffic lane to 4½ or 5 feet. This allows two people to stand side by side without crowding.

### Dining Areas

The dining area should be located near the kitchen, for obvious reasons. The dining area need not be a separate room. Although there are advantages to screening the dining area from the kitchen, an alcove that is part of the kitchen or living room saves space and allows for multiple traffic patterns. If you do choose an alcove arrangement, be sure that lighting is adequate. Plan the size of the area for the largest group that you expect to have in the dining room at one time.

Consider these key dimensions.
■ The minimum size for a table with four place settings and a buffet is 10 by 12 feet.
■ To seat eight people comfortably, you'll need an area approximately 12 by 15 feet.
■ Allow at least 24 inches of table space for each place setting; 30 inches is better.
■ Allow at least 36 inches from the edge of the table to a nearby wall to provide adequate space for seating and rising.

### Dining Area Layouts

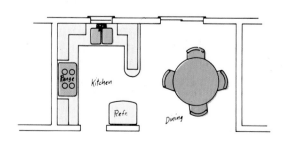

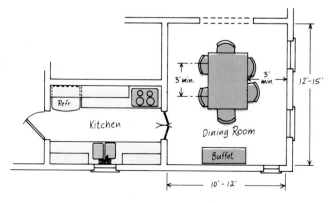

**Bedroom Layouts**

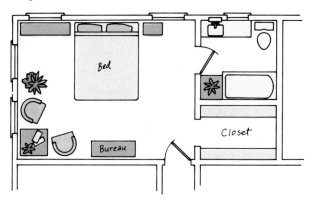

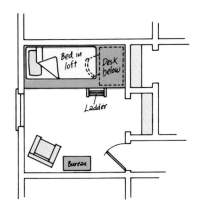

## Bedrooms

First, consider the different activity areas and functions of each bedroom. The needs for a master bedroom are obviously different than for a child's room. For instance, a master bedroom may include sitting and dressing areas, walk-in closets, and a private deck.

Unless you have a family room or play room, you may want to provide extra play space in a child's bedroom. Teenagers will need a place to study, including a desk, comfortable chair, and good lighting. You might build loft beds that create usable space underneath.

Because of drafts, beds should not be located under a window. One wall of the bedroom should be free of doors and windows to allow for the bed. Plan sufficient space on either side of the bed to accommodate a bedside table.

Here are some key dimensions.
- The minimum bedroom size is usually 70 square feet, but check your local code on this.
- Allow at least 22 inches from the edge of the bed to an adjacent wall or closet for room to make the bed.
- Allow at least 40 inches in front of a dresser or bureau to provide access to all the drawers.
- Allow at least 36 inches in front of a closet to provide access and room for dressing and grooming.

## Laundry Areas

Choose a location that is convenient and requires the fewest footsteps. Proximity to existing plumbing connections is a second important consideration. Don't overlook venting for the dryer. Check the manufacturer's recommendation for maximum distances.

The bedroom/bath area is a good choice if the walls are insulated for sound. This is where most dirty laundry accumulates and where clean laundry is stored. The bathroom is a logical location if space allows. Plumbing lines are available and the wall surfaces are moisture-resistant. The kitchen area is another popular location since this is where most homemaking activities are centered. Stacked units can help save space. Other possible locations include a bedroom hallway or a spare bedroom turned into a laundry/sewing room. In warmer climates a washer and dryer can often be located in a protected carport or breezeway.

Choose a basement location only if there is no other

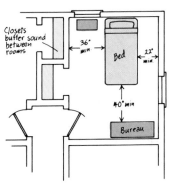

choice. This location is generally inefficient and requires too many steps up and down.

## Closets and Storage

Each person in the family should have 4 to 5 linear feet of closet space (8 to 10 square feet). All closets should have overhead lighting. Built-in closets prevent bottlenecks and simplify room layout. Keep in mind that closets do more than store clothes; they also provide a sound buffer between rooms.

The following dimensions will affect your planning.
- Closet doors should open full width if possible. A pocket door opens 100 percent, a hinged door 90 percent or more, a bifold door 66 percent, and a sliding door offers access to only 50 percent of the closet at a time.
- 24- to 30-inch depth is preferred for clothing; 16- to 20-inch depth is sufficient for linens.

**Laundry Area Layouts**

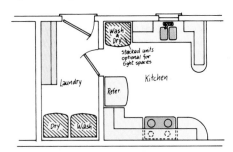

# CONCEPT PLANNING

The preceding design suggestions, together with your house inspection and priority goal list, give you the information you need to start the actual design of your remodeling. Design is both a process and an end product. The *design process* is a series of techniques used to create new ideas and to define the project.

The end product of this process is a finished design. Its first stage is a *concept plan,* which shows the general arrangement of space and how different elements of the design relate to one another. A *working plan* takes the concept plan one step farther and indicates the exact sizes, shapes, and materials to be used. The working plan, usually in blueprint form, is used by the building department and contractors for permits, estimates, and actual construction.

This section will show you how to develop a concept plan for your remodeling. If you hire a professional designer, he or she can do this for you. During your first meeting the designer will ask numerous questions about your needs and goals. Your responsibility will be to communicate as clearly as possible what you have in mind.

If you develop your own concept plan, you should still seek professional consultation and feedback.

## Should You Hire a Designer?

If your job is a major remodeling, or if you aren't entirely pleased with your concept plan, you should definitely consider hiring a professional designer—an architect, building designer, kitchen designer, or draftsman. (For a discussion of the skills and abilities of these various professionals, see the appendix.) The many advantages of hiring a professional far outweigh the cost of the services. The designer's experience can pay off in several ways: saving money on materials; simplifying construction procedures; preparing contract materials for the contractor; making sure the project meets local codes and zoning ordinances; and most important, creating an efficient and pleasing arrangement of space.

Too often the first cost-cutting move in a remodeling project is to dispense with the designer's services. In many instances this is a serious mistake. The designer's responsibility is to provide the best possible

## Zoning, Codes, and Permits

Before you begin your remodeling, it's wise to investigate several limitations that may have an impact on your plans—zoning, codes, and permits.

To learn about the legal restrictions enforced in your area, call or visit your local building department. The purpose of your visit is fact finding. You want to learn all you can about how zoning regulations and building codes will affect your plans. These laws can vary from county to county. Don't assume anything until you've checked it out.

### Zoning Regulations and Ordinances

Zoning regulations usually affect exterior construction only, not interior remodeling of existing living space. Zoning protects the quality of a neighborhood. In some areas only certain architectural styles are allowed. Ordinances can also prevent the unsuitable use of property within a specific zone. If your neighborhood is zoned for single-family houses, for example, you're protected from any business that wants to build a factory or a fast-food restaurant right next door to you.

Zoning regulations also define the required setbacks for buildings. (A setback is the specified distance a building must be from a property line.) These distances can vary from front to back and side to side. For example, the setback from the street property line may be 25 to 30 feet; on the side or adjoining property line the setback may be only 5 to 10 feet. You should know your property lines exactly. A fence or other such boundary is not an assurance of the legal property line.

There may be other special zoning requirements in your area. You'll want to find out what these are before you begin to plan in detail. For example,

your zone may have a limitation that restricts how high your building can be. This is especially important on a sloping city site.

Zoning regulations can block your plans in a number of ways. For example, if you plan a second-story addition, the restrictions may require the addition to be set back farther from the street than the first floor is. Depending on the size of your lot, this may mean that the only place you are allowed to add on is to the rear of the house. The zoning may require off-street enclosed parking for your car. If so, that affects any plans to convert your garage to living space. If you plan an addition that provides living space for your parents, the building department may interpret this as a two-family dwelling (yours and your parents'). Under existing zoning ordinances, your plans may be disallowed.

If you find that your plans conflict with the zoning regulations, you can apply for a *variance,* or exception to the law. The permit appeals department can tell you how to apply for a variance hearing if it's necessary. Once you present your case, the decision is up to the local planning board.

In addition to zoning regulations, your property may have other restrictions you should know about. For example, an *easement* gives someone else, such as the utility company or local municipality, the legal right to cross your property. A *deed restriction* may be written into your deed and limit the use of your property in some way. If you own a condominium or belong to a homeowners' association, a set of conditions, covenants, and restrictions may determine what you can do to your property. Be sure to anticipate any of these potential problems by examining your deed and checking with the building department.

design for the amount of money you have to spend. Even if your project is small or you prefer to handle the design yourself, you should have a professional designer review your concept plan. A few simple changes or suggestions at this point could save you hundreds of dollars and a lot of disappointment in the future.

## The Design Process

The techniques used in the design process are divided into three stages of activity: research, create, and critique. During the design process you will be going back and forth between these phases in a continuing cycle.

■ *Research*. This is the preliminary stage of all design. Research is simply a matter of gathering all the information you can find that pertains to your particular remodeling. For example, your research includes reading this book and others, studying product catalogs and brochures, inspecting the condition of your home, and mapping out a floor plan. It also includes a basic understanding of construction, which you can gain from the section that explains the anatomy of a house (pages 9–16). You should also look ahead to later chapters to learn more about specific building techniques necessary for your project.

■ *Create*. In this second phase, all the research you've assembled is put to use. Some of this information has an obvious, direct application to your project. Much of your research, however, is only raw material that you as the designer will transform into something totally new. Your creativity will develop new ideas and new solutions. Some of these ideas will be good, some not so good, but in this part of the process that doesn't matter. The essential task is to create as many different ideas, sketches, and plans as possible.

■ *Critique*. In this final stage, you evaluate the ideas and plans generated in phase two. This involves a conscious sorting and selecting process. You discard poor ideas and refine those which show some promise. In phase two your thinking is imaginative, fanciful, and free-wheeling; in phase three it is conservative, rational, and pragmatic. In combination, these two stages of the design process provide a natural check and balance.

### Building Codes

Local governments also decide what building codes apply in your area. The purpose of the codes is to ensure that you and others follow minimum standards for construction. Different codes may be in effect in different regions. These include the Uniform Building Code, the National Electric Code, the Uniform Mechanical Code, and the Uniform Plumbing Code, plus any state and local codes.

The building department can tell you how to obtain a copy of the appropriate code. If you're planning to do much of the work yourself, buy a copy and study it. Usually you won't need the complete code; a condensed version or guidebook can summarize the important facts you'll need to know.

The building code influences your remodeling plans by specifying the following:

■ *The type of materials that can be used*. For example, can you use plastic pipe for your plumbing? In some areas you can and in others you can't.

■ *Whether you can do the work yourself*. Some codes require electrical and plumbing work to be completed by a licensed professional.

■ *Structural requirements and installation techniques*. For example, the code will tell you how large the headers must be over doors and windows.

### Building Permits

Most remodeling projects require one or more permits before work can begin. Permits are generally needed for any alteration that changes the structure, size, safety, or use of living space. They are usually not required for projects considered to be normal maintenance such as painting, wallpapering, reroofing (unless you remove the sheathing), or window and door replacement.

But don't attempt to interpret the regulations yourself. One of the reasons for your preliminary visit to the building department is to find out the type of permits necessary for your project. Ask if inspections are necessary and at what stage of construction. Once the work begins, an inspector will visit the site to be sure that you're in compliance with the code.

Generally the code applies only to new work that's to be done. Inspections are not retroactive. If your house is old, you will probably not be expected to bring the entire structure up to code when you remodel—unless, of course, the building inspector finds something that is a definite safety hazard. Then you'll be expected to correct the situation within a reasonable amount of time. Also, improvement over a certain percentage of property value requires upgrading the whole structure to code.

You also want to find out what you need to apply for each permit. How many sets of working drawings? Can you draw the plan yourself or must they be done by a professional? If you're planning an addition that changes the exterior dimensions of your house, do you need a plot plan that shows the remodeling in relation to the property lines? If you're planning a second-story addition, do you need a structural evaluation from an eingineer to be sure the foundation is adequate to carry the load? At what stage of construction will inspection schedules be necessary? What is the permit fee? How much time is necessary from the date of application to approval? Don't assume you can get a permit on the spot as soon as you present your plans.

Remember, this is only a preliminary visit. You're seeking information that may affect your plans. It's too early to apply for a permit. That comes later, once you have finished your working plans.

## Beginning to Plan

The basic tools you'll need to develop a concept plan aren't elaborate or expensive.

■ Your project portfolio (see page 6). This includes any product literature you've filed away, as well as your list of remodeling goals. You may have expanded this into a "must/wanted" list that itemizes every feature and detail you'd like to include.

■ A pad of ¼-inch graph paper, 8½ by 11 inches or larger.

■ A pad of tracing paper, 8½ by 11 inches or larger.

■ A straightedge ruler.

■ Several soft lead pencils, and a set of colored pencils.

■ Templates for furniture, fixtures, and appliances (see page 20).

■ Optional equipment: a portable drafting table, triangles, and T-square.

■ A set of floor plans. You may be fortunate enough to have a set of your home's original blueprints. If not, use the room-by-room floor plan sketches you drew up when you surveyed your home (pages 17–19). Combine these sketches on a smaller scale to produce a plan of each floor. Don't forget to represent the thickness of the walls.

Your first remodeling plans should be rough sketches, even doodles, that merely show spaces and zones in relation to each other. From your list of goals and needs, you probably see certain groupings emerge. Represent these on paper with blobs or bubbles, linking them to each other where there should be a passageway or flow of space. You do not have to worry about scale, size, or shape.

At this point you are seeing how various functions relate to each other in terms of the space they occupy in your home. For instance, areas for eating and areas for preparing food should be close to each other, if not connected. Will you also want them connected to an entertaining area? Do you want eating areas close to sleeping areas? How do the sleeping areas relate to entertaining areas? Where should working areas be?

Experiment with many different arrangements— paper is cheap. At some point you will need to merge these bubble diagrams with the floor plan of your existing house. One way is to draw the floor plan as a bubble diagram and see how it meshes with your experimental plans. You may see a way to alter a few spaces to accommodate all your needs; or you may have to consider an extensive addition.

Your next step is to convert the bubble diagram into a more refined representation of spaces. Now the size, shape, location, and relationship of these spaces become more important. You must take into consideration the dimensions of existing rooms, the condition of your house's structure, and environmental factors like views and sunlight.

Use graph paper to speed the measuring process, choosing a convenient scale, such as a quarter-inch square to 1 foot. Then use tracing paper to refine ideas by duplicating only certain rooms or sections and trying out variations for adjacent areas.

Keep playing with various ideas, spaces, and sketches. For example, you may turn a sketch upside down and ask yourself "What if we did this?" Or you might remove all the labels from your plan and switch

## Refining Your Plans

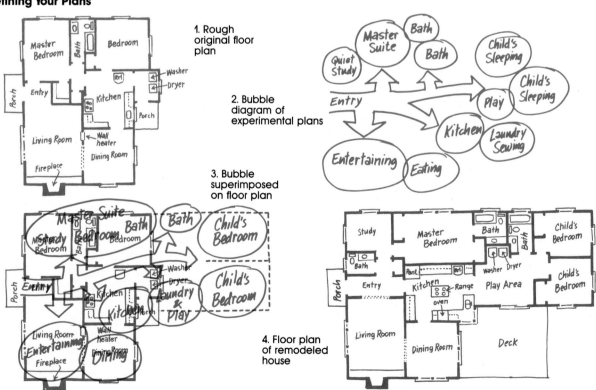

1. Rough original floor plan

2. Bubble diagram of experimental plans

3. Bubble superimposed on floor plan

4. Floor plan of remodeled house

rooms around to see what happens. Just because a room is designated as a laundry room or bedroom doesn't mean it can't serve another function as well. Remember that walls are not permanent either. Some of your most creative ideas will emerge from this type of playful attitude. Relax and have some fun while you're planning. The design process is a cycle that takes time. Don't expect to design everything in one sitting.

Gradually you'll refine your ideas to the point where one or more concepts show possibilities. Now is the time to begin incorporating dimensions and standard lumber sizes. Many building materials come in 4- by 8-foot panels; lumber is sold in 2-foot increments. Plan to use these standard sizes in your design. You should provide as much detail as you can, but it's fine if your plans remain rough at this stage of the design.

## Testing Your Plans

Use your templates to double-check space allotments. Review the key dimensions in the section on design basics to be sure you've allowed minimum spacing (see pages 19–23). You should also trace the traffic patterns on a separate overlay to see if the circulation is efficient.

Determine if your concept plan really meshes with your remodeling needs and goals. If it doesn't, refine the plan until all your requirements are satisfied. Don't compromise your goals because you haven't found a solution just yet. Keep designing until you do.

After you have created one or more concept plans that seem right, there are several techniques you can use to test them. Each of these ideas can help you visualize your plans more easily and possibly point out flaws and problems.

■ *A walk-through.* In your mind's eye simply imagine yourself walking through your plan from one end to the other. Reverse directions and walk through the space again. Concentrate on imagining yourself in each part of the room. Imagine each member of the family doing the same. You may ask other members of your household to look over your plan and imagine themselves walking through it.

■ *Interior elevations.* Doing scale drawing of each room's walls is useful for seeing how things fit and for selecting finish materials.

■ *Scale models.* Take the template concept into three dimensions. Use cardboard or balsa wood from a hobby shop to construct a simple model of your remodeling. But don't worry about details or exact sizes—it's the overall space that's important. This may take five or ten dollars in materials and an evening or two, but it can certainly be worth the effort.

■ *Masking tape and paper.* Put masking tape on the floors and walls where a new partition wall will be. You can also tape kraft or butcher paper to the ceiling to show how the space will be divided. Or hang old sheets or fabric to divide the room. Leave this up for a few days, and you'll get a good feel for what the new space will be like. Unfortunately, there is no real way of knowing what a space will be like once you tear out walls or partitions. You'll have to rely on your imagination here.

## Drawing a Rough Elevation

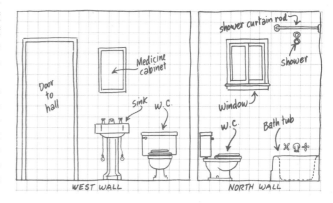

■ *Slides.* If you are planning an addition, take several slides of the exterior and project them onto drawing paper. Use the projected house to trace your old house and sketch in the form of the addition. (You can also use snapshots blown up to 4 by 5 or 8 by 10 inches.) This will help you visualize the size of the addition in proportion to the existing house.

■ *Stakes and paper.* Set up stakes at the outlines of the addition and then stand back and photograph the house and the stakes. You can also build a simple wood framework and hang paper around the frame. Cut out window and door openings and walk inside. Or put up "walls" with large sheets of corrugated cardboard. This may seem like a lot of work, but would you rather botch a $20,000 remodeling job?

If you're not sure about how your plans will look, by all means take the time to use these tools.

## The Working Plan

Your concept plans shows the general arrangement of spaces and how different elements of the design relate to one another. The dimensions may be only approximate. Before you can proceed with your project, you need to develop a set of working plans and drawings. These plans include accurate dimensions and the exact sizes and types of materials to be used. You may be able to draw these plans yourself, or you can hire a professional to do it for you.

First find out if the local code requires working plans to be professionally drawn and if any structural elements require engineering analysis. If so, you will have to contact an engineer, designer, or draftsman to provide these services (see page 93). If the building department does permit you to draw your own plans, determine how detailed they must be.

In general, provide the most complete drawings you can, including specifications for materials (see page 93). This is definitely to your advantage if you plan to hire a contractor or subcontractors for your job. Step-by-step instructions for drawing working plans are beyond the scope of this book. To learn the proper symbols and procedures you can use a drafting text such as *Architectural Drafting and Design* by Donald Hepler and Paul Wallach (McGraw-Hill, 1981).

# TAKING OUT THE OLD

Remodeling differs from new construction in one critical way—you must work with and around what is already there. Or you may need to work through it. Taking out a wall or ceiling requires knowing something about how it was put in.

In this chapter you'll learn how to become a demolition expert. That phrase may suggest an old-time war movie with John Wayne or Richard Widmark blowing up bridges somewhere in Germany. This chapter contains no dramatic explosions, however. You may send a bit of debris flying, but in most remodeling you can become an expert in demolition without detonating anything.

Demolition in remodeling simply means taking out the old in preparation for the new. In some cases that requires methodically dismantling part of your house piece by piece. In other cases demolition involves pounding out a wall or ceiling surface with a maul. If you follow the basic safety precautions, neither process is particularly dangerous or dramatic—it's just messy.

Walls are not sacred. They come down easily once you know how. The process requires some physical strength and knowledge of construction, but usually demolition can be handled by the homeowner without great skill or experience. The techniques outlined in this chapter will enable you to take out almost any surface, fixture, or wall in your home.

Demolition is a good area to save money. The cost of remodeling can be greater than that of new construction because the old has to be removed before starting the new. If you plan to hire professionals for part of your remodeling, you'll save on labor costs by preparing the job site yourself.

Of course, if you've never tackled demolition work before, some uneasiness is understandable. The prospect of tearing out a wall, for example, may seem formidable. All you have before you is a smooth plaster surface. What's behind it? Is the wall supporting your house? If so, what happens once the wall comes down?

This chapter will give you clues to identify what's likely to be inside that wall, and the information on the

anatomy of a house in Chapter 2 will alert you about what to expect. In demolition, though, you can never be certain what you're getting into until you begin the work. You can anticipate many of the problems but not all. So work carefully and cautiously. If you expect the unexpected, you will be better prepared to solve any problems that crop up.

## Planning Demolition

In demolition you must reverse the construction process, working from finish to structure, from the exposed to the hidden. Hardware and finish materials are generally removed first, then the wall and ceiling surfaces. Wiring and plumbing are removed or rerouted. Finally the exposed framing can be torn out or rebuilt.

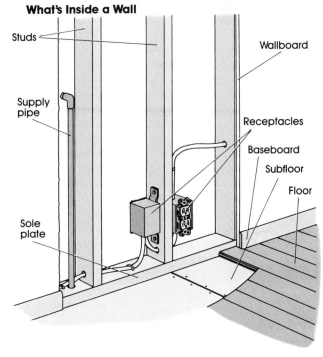

**What's Inside a Wall**

Studs

Wallboard

Supply pipe

Receptacles

Baseboard

Subfloor

Floor

Sole plate

 Removing finish materials usually takes a little skill, a few tools, and quite a bit of patience.

There are exceptions. The process can always be modified to fit the particular circumstances. If you find ways to simplify the work, fine. Practicality is the key. For example, the finish floor is usually laid last, but that doesn't mean it must always come up first. You may choose to leave it down until you have cleaned up most of the debris. The reason for this is simple. Shoveling chunks of plaster and sweeping dirt and dust is much easier over a smooth vinyl or linoleum floor than over a rough plywood or board subfloor.

Before you begin any demolition project, reevaluate your plans. Consider the consequences of any changes. If you remove a wall, will the new space become too large? How will the change affect the traffic patterns? Are the ceiling heights in the two spaces the same or compatible? Are the floor levels the same? Will you have to reroute any plumbing or heating lines?

Anticipate patching you may have to do. Ceilings usually aren't much of a problem. But what about the flooring? Will you need a threshold between existing floors? Is a completely new finish floor necessary? Do the adjacent wall surfaces match?

Once you've reviewed your plans, think through the entire demolition process several times. What are the necessary steps? What is the correct order of events? What tools will you need? You'll want to remove the old materials with a minimum of effort, so don't create unnecessary work for yourself. Often you can minimize your work load by planning ahead. There's an old saying—"measure twice, saw once." Careful measuring and cutting may enable you to open a wall for a new doorway without patching the plaster or wallboard at all. If so, you will have saved a lot of time and extra work.

In all cases protect the surrounding area and work carefully. Otherwise you can easily destroy irreplaceable woodwork or decorative details. Even if the materials can be repaired, you've only added to your list of things to do. Handle materials in large pieces whenever possible. Pulling off sections of the wall or floor in one piece is more efficient and results in less debris.

Finesse can be more important than brute strength. Some pieces have to be worried out, not overpowered. Don't go out of control with a 10-pound maul. Be methodical in your approach.

Evaluate each part of the demolition by asking "Is this step necessary?" You may be able to cover up the old material rather than expend the time and energy to remove it. If you have a lath and plaster surface in bad shape, you have two choices: rip it off and resurface the exposed studs with new wallboard or nail the new wallboard panels right over the old surface. The latter choice is especially practical for ceilings or walls that have little trim and few electrical outlets. You can locate the joists or studs, use a longer nail, and nail right through the wallboard and plaster.

If a wall has a lot of window or door trim, this cover-up approach may not be practical. The new surface adds at least 1/2 inch to the wall, so the trim must be shimmed out to accommodate the added thickness. But it's an option to consider.

Floor coverings, too, can be covered rather than removed. You can leave linoleum, vinyl tile, or hardwood floors in place and lay new flooring over them. New tile or sheet vinyl will need an underlayment of hardboard or particle board to smooth the old surface, but laying them is simple and generally faster than ripping out the old flooring first. Where old and new surfaces meet between rooms, the slight difference in height can be minimized with a step-up threshold.

**Exploring the Structure**

Before you start any demolition, you should answer two critical questions. The first and most significant is, "Will the demolition jeopardize the structural stability of the house?" The structure of your house is affected whenever you cut into or remove one of the following:
■ Bearing walls
■ Shear walls
■ Headers
■ Collar ties
■ Floor or ceiling joists
■ Rafters
■ Posts
■ Foundations

The last four situations are infrequent. If you are planning demolition work that involves cutting or removing joists, such as adding a stairway, see page 64 for details. If you want to cut or remove any rafters to add a skylight or attic dormer, see pages 77 and 81. Removing posts or foundations requires extreme caution.

**Bearing and nonbearing walls.** Before you can proceed safely, you must know the differences between bearing and nonbearing walls. In simplest terms, bearing walls hold up parts of the house. They are essential to the structure. Nonbearing or partition walls only enclose and divide the interior space.

First, assume that all exterior walls are bearing walls. Even though the end or gable walls bear less weight than the side walls, you should consider all outside walls to be bearing. Second, because not all interior walls are bearing, the problem is to identify those interior walls which help support the weight of the house.

Most homes have one main bearing wall running down the center of the house. This is because ceiling joists generally aren't strong enough to span the entire width of the house. When two joists are used, the wall where they overlap is a bearing wall.

Thus a key step in identifying bearing and nonbearing walls is to determine the direction of the floor joists or ceiling joists located above the wall. If the wall is parallel to the direction of the joists, it is probably nonbearing. If the wall is perpendicular to the joists, it is usually bearing. The best place to check the joist direction is an exposed basement or attic area, or an exposed basement ceiling area if you are removing basement walls. If this is impossible, use one of the techniques outlined in the box for locating joists and studs.

The weight a bearing wall carries must be transferred to the ground. This fact provides another clue for identifying main bearing walls: any interior wall with a

## Detecting a Bearing Wall From Beneath

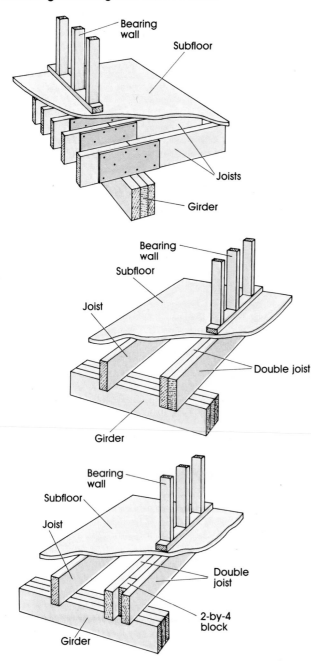

## Detecting a Bearing Wall From Above

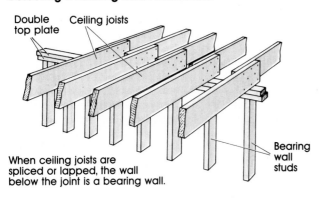

When ceiling joists are spliced or lapped, the wall below the joint is a bearing wall.

## Locating Studs and Joists

Studs and joists are sometimes difficult to locate behind finish surfaces. Although they are normally positioned 16 inches on center, in newer construction the spacing may be 24 inches, and in older homes the spacing may be irregular. So the process of finding studs and joists can be a matter of trial and error. Here are several approaches you can try.

■ Begin by measuring 16 inches from the wall or ceiling corner. Rap the surface with your knuckles until you hear a solid sound. If it sounds hollow, try again on either side. This method works best with wallboard surfaces, but not so well with lath and plaster.

■ Note the nail locations on the baseboard or wall paneling. These nails are usually driven into studs.

■ Use a small drill bit or nail to make a hole in the wall or ceiling where you think the stud or joist should be. If you don't hit one, try again on either side. You may have to make several holes, but if they are small and located near the baseboard or ceiling line, they are easily patched. You can also insert a thin wire into the hole and probe to either side until you locate the stud or joist. Or drive a small nail completely through the ceiling or floor surface. In the basement or attic, measure the distance from the nail to the nearest joist.

■ Use a magnetic stud finder. The magnetized pointer will waver when it passes over metal. Any nails driven into the studs or joists should cause the pointer to move. These devices are inexpensive, but they're not foolproof.

### Locating Studs and Joists

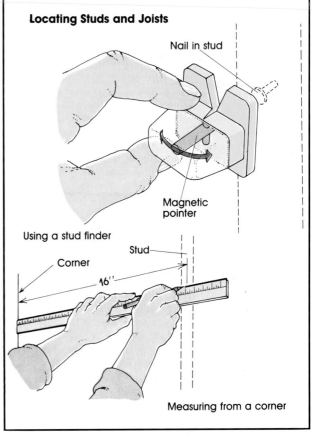

girder, post, or foundation beneath it is probably bearing. In a building of two or more stories, these bearing walls are usually stacked on top of one another.

Of course, all rules and guidelines have exceptions. Short sections of wall around a closet, for example, may be perpendicular to the joists but aren't necessarily bearing. If you have a central hallway running the length of your house, one wall is probably the main bearing wall. (In the attic, check where the ceiling joists overlap.) Depending on the size of the joists, the other hallway wall may carry only a small portion of the load.

Another exception to look for is the use of strongbacks in the attic. The strongback is a board set on edge, or even a beam, that runs perpendicular to the joists in the middle of their span. Typical construction is a flat 2 by 4 nailed to the joists, with a 2 by 8 or 2 by 10 set on edge and nailed alongside the 2 by 4. It looks like the strongback is resting on the joists, but in fact it is helping support them. Its two ends, or even points along its length, bear on walls below, like a bridge supported by its piers.

The purpose of the strongback is twofold: to straighten the joists during framing and to prevent long joist spans from sagging once the finish ceiling is applied. The weight of the strongback, and of the joists, is supported by the walls at each end. As a result any wall directly beneath a strongback should be treated as a secondary bearing wall. In some cases strongbacks also help to support the rafters, which means additional weight is transferred to the walls below.

**Inside the walls.** The second question to answer before starting any demolition is, "What's inside?" Although you can never answer this question completely, it's important to have some idea of what to expect before you begin.

### Construction of a Strongback

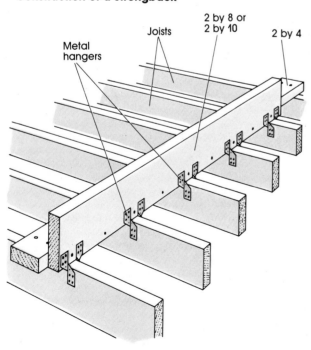

Metal hangers
Joists
2 by 8 or 2 by 10
2 by 4

Don't tear out any wall, floor, ceiling, or cabinetry without first looking for clues. You're likely to find one or more of the following:
- Electrical wiring
- Water supply or DWV plumbing pipes
- Pipes and ducts for the heating system
- Gas pipes
- Abandoned wiring, pipes, vents, and flues
- Insulation

Before any demolition do some detective work. Note the location of all electrical switches and outlets in the area. The attic may reveal the location of electrical wiring. In most demolitions electrical wiring can be pulled out or rerouted easily. You may be able to do this yourself, or you can hire an electrician.

Go down in the basement and look for pipes and ducts that run in the vicinity. The proximity of the kitchen and bath will give you clues about the location of the supply and drain pipes. If the area includes plumbing or heating pipes, avoid unnecessary rerouting if you can. Of course, it's not impossible to remove or reroute the lines, but the job can be more complicated and expensive than you might imagine. So if you are unsure, call a plumber or heating contractor to take a look.

■*A word of caution:* If the demolition area involves any natural gas lines, call a professional. If you discover what you suspect is a gas line during demolition, stop work immediately and seek expert advice. Inadvertent damage to the pipe could have dangerous consequences. This is one area that should be handled only by an experienced professional.

### Salvage and Debris
In many demolition projects you'll be faced with the dilemma of salvaging materials. The question of whether to save or not to save is best answered on a case-by-case basis. Some items can be salvaged easily; others represent a complete waste of time. When to salvage is primarily a matter of judgment.

**What to save.** There are four main reasons for salvaging existing materials.

■ *For resale value.* Although few built-in fixtures or materials in the average home have resale value, don't automatically assume everything is worthless. What is junk to you may be a valuable antique to others. Age is usually the determining factor. If your home is more than thirty years old, you may have items worth selling.

If you're removing old plumbing fixtures such as a Victorian pedestal sink or clawfoot tub, call several salvage yards or antique dealers to find out if they're interested. The same is true of decorative bath accessories, light fixtures, and door knobs. Brass electrical plates may have salvage value. Even if your plumbing fixtures aren't antiques, inquire about their value before you rip them out. You may not be offered much, but selling them can save you the time and expense of hauling them away yourself.

Some metals have resale value. Old radiators and cast iron plumbing fixtures, for example, can be sold for scrap metal. Copper and brass plumbing can be recycled. Copper wiring, however, isn't worth much unless you have a lot of it, or large-diameter wires.

Large timber beams and expensive wood paneling have value if they can be salvaged easily. In some areas salvage dealers are interested in used hardwood flooring. Before you go ahead, though, weigh the offered price against the time it will take to remove it carefully enough for salvage.

■ *For future use.* To salvage materials for your own future use, all you need is sufficient space to store them safely. Be sure the storage area is dry, protected from vermin, and out of the way so materials won't get broken or scarred before reuse.

■ *For use on the present job.* You'll want to salvage materials for possible use on the present job for two reasons. First, you may need some of the old material for patching or repair. For example, if you're removing only part of a wall or floor, save some of the finish material if you can. If you inadvertently damage the remaining finish, you'll have extra pieces for patching. Saving some of the lumber from an older home can be useful. Often the dimensions are different from present-day lumber, and you just can't buy matching stock anymore.

Second, your plans could change halfway through the project. In that case you might be happy to have some of the old material on hand. As a rule of thumb, if something can be saved easily, save it.

■ *For its esthetic value.* Salvage is often a matter of taste and preference. If you like the style and appearance of the old material, save it. Even if it's not cost-effective, you may decide it's worth saving.

**What not to save.** In some situations, of course, salvaging is neither practical nor desirable. Your goal is maximum value for minimum effort. If you're going to remove a surface completely and start over, you may not need to bother with salvage. If new materials of comparable or superior quality are readily available for reasonable cost, it's probably better to replace the old with the new. Investigate the cost of new materials and then decide. Salvaging isn't always cost-effective. Sometimes you'll have to spend too much time cleaning up the old material for reuse.

If you are planning to hire professionals to do some of the work, think twice about using salvaged materials. Most professionals don't like working with used goods. New materials are faster and easier and offer fewer surprises. The more time spent trying to repair the old, the more the labor will cost. You may have to rely on the contractor's judgment here.

Even when you're doing the work yourself, be practical about saving old materials. Your time is worth something, too. For example, it's usually not sensible to try to save small sections of lath and plaster if you are installing new wallboard anyway. If a section is left under a new window or 2 feet at the end of a wall, go ahead and rip it out. It's faster and easier to put up another piece of wallboard than to try to patch the old plaster and new wallboard together.

Often the same is true of old plumbing. In many instances it's more practical to run new copper or plastic pipe than to take the time to patch and rejoin existing galvanized and cast iron pipe.

If what you find is obviously not right, it's usually better to rip it out and start fresh. For example, it's sensible to replace a jerry-built wall that has unorthodox framing or spacing between the studs, or unconventional wiring and plumbing installations.

**Dealing with debris.** In thinking through the entire demolition process, it's easy to overlook the final step—what to do with the debris. You should make the necessary provisions for handling and hauling the rubble before you begin any demolition work.

As a rule of thumb, 1 square foot of wall area results in approximately 1 cubic foot of debris. This can be quite heavy. Don't use boxes or containers that are too large or pack them too tight. Consider buying or renting a wheelbarrow to speed the removal process. You can also save yourself a lot of backbreaking labor by building a temporary chute or slide to get the debris outside.

If you're going to set aside some materials for future use, prepare a convenient storage area before any demolition begins. The location should be easy to reach but well out of the work area. This could be a garage, basement, or back porch.

In most communities the municipal garbage system won't pick up debris from a remodeling project. Although it's worth a phone call to find out, many areas have stringent limits on the weight and number of extra containers allowed.

If you're going to do a lot of demolition, the practical solution is to rent a dumpster. The cost is a daily or weekly rental fee, plus a charge for each pickup. In some communities a permit is necessary to leave the dumpster on the street. Check with your local building department on this.

If the job isn't large enough to warrant a dumpster, you can rent a trailer or pickup truck and cart the junk away yourself. When comparing costs, don't overlook the cost of gas and municipal dump fees you'll have to pay. Also keep in mind that hauling debris takes time. You may decide it would be more cost-effective to stay on the job site and pay for someone else to remove the debris. You might get bids from high school or college students who run a weekend hauling business.

## Preparing the Work Area

Demolition can be a dirty job, especially if you're removing plaster or wallboard surfaces. Seal off the room and confine the mess to one area if you can. This keeps the rest of the house livable, and you spend less time cleaning up. If you're taking out a wall, prepare the rooms on either side. Open windows in the work area to provide plenty of ventilation, but close others throughout the house to keep dust from coming in. Hang canvas, old linens, or plastic sheets over doorways to the work area.

Be sure to protect any finish surfaces you want to keep. Porous wall surfaces such as wallpaper should be covered with sheets of thin plastic. If you want to save the finish flooring, put down building paper, canvas drop

# FINISH MATERIALS

cloths, plastic sheets, or an old rug turned upside down. A large tarpaulin that can be picked up and carried outside is convenient, but put plastic sheets underneath. Another good system is a layer of plastic covered with building paper. Plastic alone isn't strong enough and tears easily. Building paper alone doesn't keep the fine dust out of the cracks and seams in the flooring. (Once there, it's practically impossible to remove—you'll see it forever.) Tape the edges of the building paper to keep the debris from working underneath. Plaster and wallboard particles are gritty and will quickly mar finish floors if ground in.

If you're going to remove the ceiling surface, put down several sheets of inexpensive 1/4-inch CDX grade plywood or old carpet over the building paper. This will prevent large jagged pieces of plaster or wallboard from gouging the finish floor.

You need to protect yourself as well as your house. Always dress appropriately for demolition work. This means long sleeves, gloves, and heavy work shoes—no canvas or running shoes. For overhead work a hard hat is recommended. Use goggles to protect your eyes from flying debris. If there's any dust, especially plaster dust, wear a mask. Throw-away paper masks are adequate; a mask with replaceable filters is much better.

If your demolition project involves electrical wiring, turn off the appropriate circuits before you begin. You don't want any live wire surprises once you start swinging a sledge or cutting through walls with a saw. Shut off everything in the vicinity, even if you don't plan to touch the wiring. You never know exactly where the wires run until you get inside the wall or ceiling. Use a long, heavy-duty extension cord to provide electricity to power tools and portable lights.

To identify which circuits need to be turned off, refer to the circuit map in your service panel (page 13). Many rooms are wired on several circuits, so don't assume one dead outlet means the entire room is dead. Use a voltage tester or night light to be sure all outlets and switches in the area are off.

If the area involves plumbing lines, locate the appropriate shutoff valves for the branch run or fixture. Even if you don't plan to remove the pipes, shut off the water supply before you begin. Mistakes do happen. If the water is turned off first, you'll avoid sudden floods.

Plan to clean the area often during demolition. Don't let accumulated debris interfere with the work in progress or create a safety hazard. Carry the rubble outside regularly. Otherwise you might stumble over it and cut yourself on nails or jagged pieces of lath and plaster. Also, excessive plaster dust in the air can irritate the eyes and lungs.

As an added safety precaution, remove or flatten all nails from each piece of trim or framing material as it comes down. Protruding nails can easily rip your clothes or skin. Without them, handling and stacking the pieces is more convenient. Although some demolition veterans may not take the time, this additional precaution is a sound idea. Your safety is more important than a few minutes of your time.

## Removing Finish Materials

Whether you want to remove a medicine cabinet or knock out part of the wall between your living room and dining room, all the planning and preparation you've done will pay off once you pick up your tools. In this section you'll find instructions for removing wood trim, doors and frames, sinks, washbasins, toilets, bathtubs, cabinets, and built-ins. You will also see how to remove sections of lath and plaster, wallboard, wood paneling, and ceramic tile, hardwood flooring, resilient tiles, linoleum, sheet vinyl, and carpeting.

## Wood Trim

First examine the trim and determine the original installation sequence. Then reverse the order. If you want to save the trim, use a flat bar to pry the piece gently from the wall. You may need to sever the wall surface from the trim by scoring with a utility knife. If the wall or ceiling is to be saved, protect the surface by using a wood block wrapped in cloth behind the head of the pry bar. You may be able to drive the finish nails through the trim with a nail set. This is especially true for mitered casings around doors and windows that have been nailed through the corners. Immediately remove any nails from trim to be saved. Otherwise the pieces may be gouged or scratched before reuse. Often nails can be pulled through from the back or cut off with nippers so the face isn't marred at all.

If you don't intend to save the trim, rip it off with a wrecking bar. Flatten the nails for safety and easier handling. If wood trim is glued as well as nailed in place, it's impossible to salvage much.

**Removing Trim**

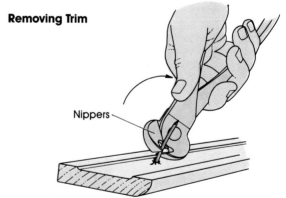

Nippers

## Doors and Frames

If you wish to salvage any hardware, remove it carefully first. Then remove the door from the frame by tapping out the hinge pins. Remove the trim and casings as just outlined. In some cases you can remove the jambs by prying from the bottom. If the finish floor interferes, an alternative technique is to cut through the side jambs and remove them by sections. If you intend to save the jambs, cut the nails holding them to the studs. If the nails are hidden by shim stock, tap it out with a chisel or flat bar. Once the nails are visible, cut them with a hacksaw blade or place the V end of a pry bar over the nail and rap sharply with a hammer to shear the nails. Then lift or pry the frame carefully from the rough opening.

**Removing a Door Frame**

Door casing
Wood block
Wrecking bar
Header
Jamb
Shim
Wrecking bar
Edge of plaster or wallboard
Edge of painted area
Stud

## Sinks and Basins

There are three types of sinks and washbasins: built-ins, wall-hung models, and pedestal sinks. The demolition process is similar for all three.

First shut off the water supply. You will probably find two shutoff valves beneath the fixture or the nearest branch line. Disconnect the waste line from the sink by removing the slip nut with a wrench. If you can reuse the trap, leave it in place; otherwise remove it. Be sure to cover the trap or exposed drain line to keep debris from entering the waste system and to keep sewer gases from entering the house. Stuff the end of the pipe with paper or cover with a plastic bag and tape it down. Next disconnect the supply lines from the sink and cover the ends.

If the sink is built-in, temporarily brace it from below by nailing across a scrap 2 by 4. If the sink is tiled in with ceramic tile, chip away some tiles with a chisel to free the sink. (For information on removing tile, see page 38.) Remove any screws that clamp the sink to the counter-top and lift the sink out.

Wall-mounted sinks are hung by a hanger bar or brackets from a support screwed into the studs. After disconnecting the plumbing, lift one side of the sink at a time up and away from the wall.

If the sink is a pedestal model, disconnect the plumbing and any bolts securing the pedestal. If the pedestal is cemented to the floor, rock it back and forth to break the bond. For more detailed information on removing plumbing fixtures, see Ortho's book *Basic Plumbing Techniques*.

## Toilets

First shut off the water supply and flush the toilet. Remove as much water as possible from the bowl with a sponge. Next disconnect the supply pipe. Cover the ends to keep debris from entering the supply system.

If the tank and bowl are separate units, disconnect the elbow connecting them. If the tank is attached to the wall with hanger bolts, prop it temporarily with scrap wood or have a helper hold it while you remove the

bolts. If the tank is bolted to the bowl, as in newer toilets, remove the bolts and lift the tank out. Next remove the nuts connecting the bowl to the floor. Break the seal between the toilet and the drain pipe by rocking the bowl back and forth from side to side. Because the built-in trap inside the bowl is filled with water, lift the bowl straight up if you can. To keep debris out of the waste line and sewer gases in, stuff newspapers or rags into the drain pipe and cover with a plastic bag.

## Bathtubs

Taking out a tub isn't quite as simple as removing a sink or toilet. Often it's a job best left to professionals, unless the tub is an old free-standing model. In that case the plumbing lines are exposed and can be easily disconnected. Modern tubs, however, are usually built into the surrounding walls, which means you must take off part of the wall surface before you can remove the tub. Before you begin, measure the tub. If it won't fit through the existing doorway, you may have to remove part of the wall framing. Another option with a cast iron tub is to break it up with a sledge hammer.

The first step in removing a tub is to remove the fixture hardware, such as the spigot and faucet handles. Next you need access to the drain and supply lines. Check the wall surface in the room opposite the end of the tub. If you're lucky, you will find an access panel. Remove it, shut off the water supply, and disconnect the drain and supply pipes. If there's no panel, you'll have to cut into the wall surface to gain access. Before you do this be sure to shut off the nearest water supply, such as the branch run. When cutting into the wall, be careful not to damage the plumbing. Once you've gained access disconnect the supply and waste lines. If the tub is surrounded by ceramic tile, remove at least the bottom course, plus any mortar bed or wallboard behind the tile. Once the studs are exposed, remove any nails or screws that connect the tub flanges to the wall. Then the tub can be lifted and carried from the room. If the tub is cast iron, it's going to be heavy—you may need three or four people to get it out.

## Cabinets and Built-ins

The type of cabinetry determines the demolition process. Manufactured cabinets usually can be removed intact without much trouble. Unless they are solid or exotic wood, used cabinets have little resale value. If you intend to reuse them elsewhere in the house, such as in a workshop or garage, you'll obviously want to exercise more care than if you're throwing them away.

Start with the base cabinets. If a sink is involved, remove it first by following the steps outlined on page 35. If the counter and backsplash are covered with plastic laminate, you should be able to remove the entire wood framework in one piece. Remove any screws or nails that connect it to the base cabinets and lift it off. If the counter is ceramic tile, follow the instructions on page 38 for removing tile.

Next examine the base cabinets to see how they are attached to the wall. Most manufactured cabinets are screwed to the wall and to each other. Removing the doors is optional at this point. If you intend to reuse the cabinets, removing the doors first may lessen the chance of damage when you carry them out. If you have someone to help carry, as well as sufficient clearance, it's possible to take out several units at one time. Remove the screws that attach the cabinets to the wall, but leave the side screws in place. If you're doing the job alone, however, remove the wall and side screws and carry out each unit separately.

For the upper cabinets follow the same procedure, with one exception. Before you remove any screws, prop the cabinets with a number of 2-by-4 legs for support. You can also nail a 2 by 4 to the wall beneath the cabinets to provide temporary support.

Old-style cabinets that are built in place generally have to be demolished. It's not practical to disassemble them piece by piece and rebuild them elsewhere. First remove any trim between the ceiling and wall surfaces. Next determine how the cabinets are attached to the wall. If you can locate any screws or nails that mount the back of the cabinets to the wall, remove them. You may be able to pull the cabinets down in one piece. Otherwise use a wrecking bar to rip the cabinets apart. In older homes cabinets were often installed before the walls were finished with plaster. As a result you may have to resurface the studs with wallboard before you can put up new cabinetry.

## Lath and Plaster

You can use several tools and techniques to remove lath and plaster. Although power tools can be used in some instances, hand tools are generally better. All the techniques result in dirty, messy work—there's no escaping that.

If you are removing just a section of plaster, it's important to cut it cleanly from the surfaces to be saved. Otherwise large portions of the wall or ceiling you intend to save will be pulled away during demolition. Prepare for the cut by marking an outline, with pencil, of the section to be removed. Then place masking tape along the side of the line where plaster is to be saved. Start the cut by scoring along the pencil line with a sharp utility knife. The deeper the cut the better. You can also use a masonry chisel with a broad blade. Next use a wrecking bar, maul, or claw hammer to knock down the plaster. Rip off all the plaster first, remove it from the room, and then pull off the lath. It's easier to shovel up the plaster before the lath is mixed in with it. Work carefully around any plumbing or wiring. To reach the ceiling use a step ladder or build a simple scaffold with planks. With ceiling surfaces all you can do is rip and duck, so be sure to wear your goggles, hard hat, and mask.

If you want to speed the cutting process, you can try a reciprocating saw or circular saw with a masonry blade. But be forewarned: for this job you're better off sticking with hand tools. With the reciprocating saw the motion of the blade causes the lath to vibrate, and chunks of plaster you intended to save will be knocked down. With a circular saw the blade kicks up so much plaster dust that your work area is totally obscured within a matter of minutes. Some installations use metal lath or at least a metal edge strip along the inside and outside corners. Use a cold chisel to pound this out, or cut the metal with tin snips.

If you are removing only part of the wall or ceiling,

### Removing Cabinets to Save

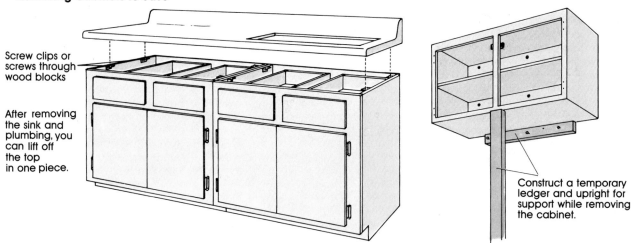

Screw clips or screws through wood blocks

After removing the sink and plumbing, you can lift off the top in one piece.

Construct a temporary ledger and upright for support while removing the cabinet.

## Removing a Section of Lath and Plaster

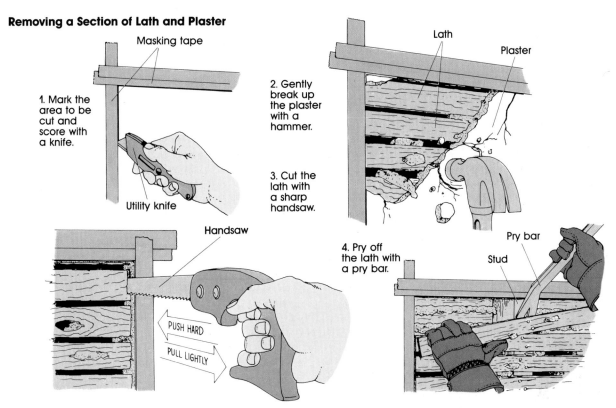

1. Mark the area to be cut and score with a knife.

Masking tape

Utility knife

2. Gently break up the plaster with a hammer.

3. Cut the lath with a sharp handsaw.

Lath

Plaster

Handsaw

PUSH HARD

PULL LIGHTLY

4. Pry off the lath with a pry bar.

Pry bar

Stud

cut next to a stud or joist if possible. If you cut between them, the unsupported plaster will vibrate and break in a jagged line. To make a small opening in lath and plaster (for an access panel or electrical outlet), first drill a small starter hole. Then use a keyhole saw to cut the opening. If it's not possible to cut near a stud or joist, use short, deliberate strokes to prevent the plaster from breaking unevenly.

If you are going to do any patching, save some of the longer pieces of lath. You may also need them to fur out the studs before you install new wallboard. Save whatever lath you can, within practical limits. Buying new lath for furring is not that expensive.

Carry the debris outside frequently. If you pull down the whole wall or ceiling and then try to clean up, you'll have an impossible mess.

### Wallboard

The techniques and tools used for removing wallboard are essentially the same as those used for lath and plaster, except that the process is easier, quicker, and less messy. In most wallboard installations the ceiling panels are put up first, then the walls. In demolition reverse the order and remove the walls first. With some practice you will be able to pull off large pieces of wallboard from stud to stud or joist to joist, but even large sections have no salvage value. New wallboard is so inexpensive it's not worth saving any of the old.

If the panels have been glued and nailed to the studs, use a chisel or wood scraper to remove small pieces stuck to the studs. To remove only a single 4-by-8 panel, cut the paper seam between the panels with a sharp utility knife. If pulling the panel starts to damage

the adjoining surfaces, try to find the nail heads and drive them through with a nail set.

### Wood Paneling

First remove any trim along the baseboard and corners. If the paneling is composed of individual boards, use a flat bar to pull each board away from the studs or furring strips. You may have to damage the first piece to gain access.

With 4-by-8 plywood panels, use a nail set to drive the nails through the paneling. Or you can try prying the edge of the panel from a stud—the nails may pull through easily. Generally there's a small gap between the floor and bottom edge for acces. If the panels are only nailed to the wall, they can be salvaged without much difficulty, but if the panels are nailed and glued, salvage is practically impossible. The glue bond is so strong the wood will tear and rip. Unfortunately the most expensive paneling—the type you most want to save— is usually glued and therefore unsalvageable.

### Hardwood Flooring

Old hardwood floors are usually refinished or covered with carpeting or other material. In some cases, however, you may need to remove the old hardwood flooring. If you want to save any sections of the floor, number the back of each piece as it comes up. This makes relaying much easier. If you have other hardwood floors in the house, save some pieces for future repairs. Otherwise you may have a difficult time finding a good match.

Begin by removing the baseboard trim. If there's a gap between the first piece and the wall, use a pry bar

### Removing Tongue-and-Groove Flooring

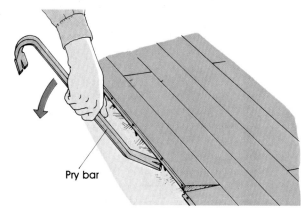

Pry bar

to pull it up. If there's no access, you may have to use a wood chisel or circular saw to cut the first piece. Set the saw to the depth of the finish floor and use a utility blade. Once the first board is out, the others should pry up easily. Tongue-and-groove (T&G) flooring will take more care than boards that are shiplapped or face-nailed. The boards are nailed through the tongues, so be sure to pry from that side.

Wood flooring is occasionally nailed over the joists without a subfloor. This practice leaves you three options: protect the finish floor and wait until the rest of the demolition is completed to refinish it, remove and replace it with a stronger subfloor before work begins, or cover it with particle-board underlayment before putting down new vinyl flooring.

### Ceramic Tile

Removing ceramic tile depends on the type of installation. In older homes the tile is almost always laid on a ¾-inch- or 1-inch-thick mortar bed, which is essentially reinforced concrete. Because it lasts so long, this type of installation is still used in new construction. In many newer homes, though, ceramic tile is set with mastic on a plywood or wallboard backing.

If you're going to remove the entire wall, there's no need to save any tile. With a mortar bed use a maul to pound out both tile and mortar. Keep in mind that some walls have plumbing connections behind them, so don't be overly zealous. Be sure to wear goggles to protect your eyes from flying chips. The dust can be irritating, too, so wear a mask. To cut away whole chunks at a time, use a circular saw with a masonry blade. The saw will kick up even more debris, so be careful.

If the backing is plywood or wallboard, pound out the entire wall or chip the tiles away and then remove the backing. Generally plywood or wallboard will be gouged and chipped so badly it will have to be replaced. Don't try to save it.

To remove only a few tiles, you can smash each tile with a hammer and then chip out the pieces. Or use a masonry chisel and chip around the edges of each tile. If you want to save any for patching, proceed slowly and learn as you go. Use a lot of light taps instead of solid blows. You may lose the first four or five tiles until you find an approach that works for you.

### Removing Ceramic Tile

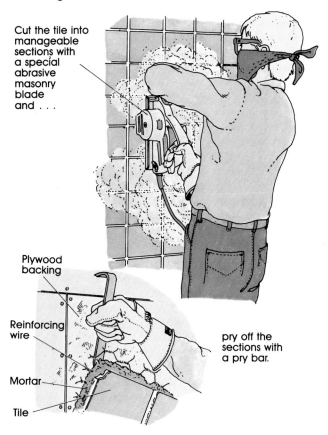

Cut the tile into manageable sections with a special abrasive masonry blade and . . .

Plywood backing

Reinforcing wire

Mortar

Tile

pry off the sections with a pry bar.

### Resilient Tile

First remove all the baseboard trim. If you want to save the tiles, applying heat makes removal easier. Use a propane torch, or an iron over a sheet of aluminum foil. When the tile has softened, slip a putty knife under the edge and lift. If you're not saving any tiles, chip them out with a stiff putty knife or chisel. A flat bar or a long-handled scraper with a flat blade also works well. If you're lucky, the tiles are glued to building paper, and both materials will come up together. If the tiles are glued to a particle board or a hardwood floor, the job of chipping and lifting is more tedious.

In the case of underlayment, it may be easier to saw the tiles and underlayment into 4-by-4 squares. Using a circular saw, set the blade depth so it will cut through the particle board but not into the subfloor. Pry up the large squares and remove them. New particle board underlayment will have to be nailed down to the subfloor if you plan to use tiles or sheet flooring.

Remove any mastic stuck to the subfloor after the tiles are up. Some mastics dissolve with acetone or mineral spirits. Be sure to use these with adequate ventilation. *Under no circumstances should you use kerosene or gasoline, which are extreme fire hazards.* If nothing dissolves the mastic, use a scraper to get it off. If only a little mastic remains, sand it smooth with a power sander. The process can be expensive, though, since the mastic quickly gums and destroys sanding belts.

## Removing Resilient Tile

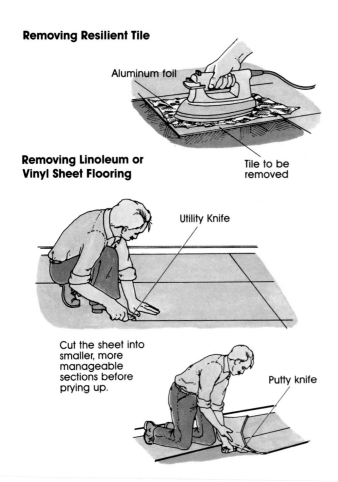

Aluminum foil

Tile to be removed

## Removing Linoleum or Vinyl Sheet Flooring

Utility Knife

Cut the sheet into smaller, more manageable sections before prying up.

Putty knife

## Linoleum and Sheet Vinyl

These two materials are similar to resilient tile. Both are glued with mastic over a variety of underlayments, such as felt, building paper, hardboard, or plywood. First try cutting the flooring into strips with a utility knife and pulling up a section at a time. This may not be possible if the flooring is old and brittle. If it breaks into small pieces, follow the procedure just outlined for removing resilient tiles. Often it's faster to cover the old floor with a new underlayment and finish floor.

## Carpeting

Carpeting is generally attached to the floor with tack strips around the perimeter of the room. These strips are narrow pieces of thin cardboard or wood embedded with rows of nailing tacks. You may be able to grip the carpet at one edge and pull it up by hand or to insert a pry bar to lift the tack strip from the floor. In any case removing the carpeting itself is not the major problem— it's the foam or felt padding underneath that's likely to give you the most difficulty. If the padding is stapled to the floor, it pulls up easily, but the staples stay behind and have to be removed one by one. If the padding is glued to the subfloor with mastic, much of it will fall apart when you try to pull it up, so follow the procedures outlined earlier for scraping and lifting resilient tile. Although carpeting can often be used elsewhere, padding is generally so compressed and torn up that it's impossible to reuse.

Once the surface materials have been completely removed, electrical, plumbing, and heating systems are exposed and accessible. At this point you can evaluate what you've got and decide whether to reroute or remove them.

## Electrical Wiring

Before you disconnect any wiring, be certain the current is shut off for that particular circuit. Use a voltage tester on all wires to check for power. If the entire circuit is to be removed, the problem is solved simply. First pull the main switch to shut off all power coming into the house. Next disconnect the circuit's wiring from the service panel. Then remove all switches, outlets, and junction boxes for that circuit. If possible, pull out all wires.

In most cases you need not remove an entire circuit, but only individual outlets and switches. If an outlet to be removed has only one cable coming into the box (which means two wires, one black and one white), it's wired at the end of the run. Trace the cable back to the nearest box, disconnect it from both boxes, and pull it out. If the outlet box has two incoming cables (four wires), it's wired in the middle of the run.

If you intend to save any outlets or switches connected on either side, first disconnect and pull out the unneeded cable. Then, if possible, reroute the remaining cables to a new location. This often requires pulling the wiring behind existing wall or floor surfaces with a fish tape. (For information on running electrical cable see page 52.) If the cable isn't long enough, pull it out and start over with new unspliced cable. The electrical code demands that all connections be made inside ap-

## Using a Voltage Tester

A voltage tester has no power of its own but tests for the presence of power in wires or appliances. Use it to be sure the power is off before making repairs, to see if an outlet is hot, or to test for proper grounding.

To test for power at an outlet, put one probe in each slot.

proved outlet or junction boxes, which must be accessible, not hidden behind a finish surface.

If the wiring involved is particularly complex, consult Ortho's book *Basic Wiring Techniques* for additional information. Or call an electrician to sort out the problem. In many instances you can pull the wiring to one side, proceed with the demolition, and have the electrician reroute the system later.

### Plumbing and Heating Pipes

Rerouting plumbing and heating pipes generally requires removing all or portions of the old system and then running new lines. The existing pipes can't be pushed or pulled into new locations, so you don't have the same flexibility as with electrical wiring. Occasionally pieces of the old system can be salvaged and reused. That depends on the type and condition of the material.

Often you can save money by doing the preparatory work yourself. This chapter describes how to remove various types of pipes, ducts, and heating fixtures you may encounter. Instructions for installing new plumbing lines, however, are beyond the scope of this book. For that you should consult Ortho's book *Basic Plumbing Techniques* or call a professional.

Before you remove any water pipes, shut off the supply to the branch run. Then locate the appropriate drain valve and remove the water from the pipe.

■ *Copper pipe.* Pipes connected with flare fittings can be disassembled with two wrenches. If the pipe has soldered fittings, cut it with a tube cutter or fine hacksaw blade. You can also disassemble soldered fittings by heating them with a propane torch if there's enough room. Once the solder melts, pull the fittings apart.

■ *Plastic pipe.* The cement between plastic fittings is so strong that disassembling is impossible, so cut the pipe near the fittings with a hacksaw blade. Long lengths of pipe in good condition can be reused. Fittings must be thrown away.

■ *Galvanized pipe.* Cut galvanized pipe with a hacksaw. Because the pipe is heavier than either copper or plastic, you may need to brace a long length to keep the saw blade from binding. Use pipe wrenches to disassemble unions and other fittings. If the pipe is so corroded that it's frozen solid, try putting an extra length of pipe over the wrench handle to gain greater leverage. Or expand the fittings by heating with a propane torch. Lubricating oil may also help loosen the fittings.

■ *Cast iron pipe.* If the cast iron is hubless, you may have enough space to disassemble the clamps and couplings. If there is no access, or the cast iron is joined with lead and oakum, you'll need to rent a chain pipe cutter. You can also try chipping the lead and pulling out the oakum, although usually there isn't enough room to pull the pipes apart. Another way to cut cast iron pipe is with a power circular saw and a special metal cutoff blade. The disc-shaped blade, which has no teeth, fits on the saw like a regular blade. It creates a lot of sparks but works very well.

■ *Heating ducts.* Sheet metal ducts can be cut easily with tin snips. You may need to drill or punch a hole first to gain access. Some runs can be disassembled by removing the connecting sheet metal screws. Rerouting is generally a job for a professional. Not only does estimating the proper heating capacity require specialized knowledge, but fabricating the new ductwork requires a professional's tools.

■ *Radiators.* The entire system must be drained back to the boiler. Then disconnect the pipes and lift the radiator out. Cut and cap the pipes at the joists or remove them completely, whichever is more convenient.

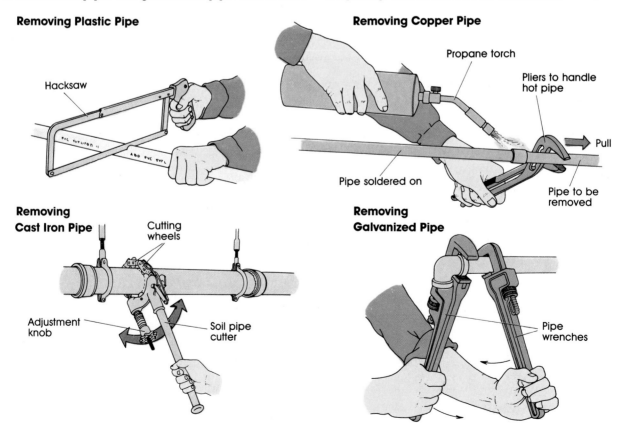

**Removing Plastic Pipe**

Hacksaw

**Removing Copper Pipe**

Propane torch

Pliers to handle hot pipe

Pull

Pipe soldered on

Pipe to be removed

**Removing Cast Iron Pipe**

Cutting wheels

Adjustment knob

Soil pipe cutter

**Removing Galvanized Pipe**

Pipe wrenches

# REMOVING WALLS

All that now remains is the wood framing. Having already examined the structural framework (see page 17), you should start by removing the partition walls.

## Nonbearing Walls

Taking out a nonbearing wall is relatively simple. Begin by taking out the studs. The proper technique for this depends on two factors: how the studs are nailed to the plates and whether you plan to save them. To remove the studs in one piece takes more time, but you may decide it's worth it. (See the discussion on salvaging materials, page 32.)

If the studs are end-nailed through the top plate and toenailed to the sole plate, use a nail puller or wrecking bar to pull out the toenails. Once the lower end is free, grasp the stud in the middle and twist and pry it loose from the top plate. Be careful not to damage any ceiling surfaces you want to save.

If the studs are end-nailed to both top and sole plates, it may be impossible to remove them without damage. You can try pounding the base of the stud with a maul, but this often results in breaking or splintering the wood. Or you can use a reciprocating saw with a utility blade and cut through both wood and nails at the base of the stud.

If you choose not to save the studs, smash them out with a maul. Or you can cut them in half with a reciprocating or circular saw. (Be careful of saw kickback as you finish your cut.) Then twist and pry out both ends. Be sure to remove or flatten any protruding nails once the studs are down.

After the studs are out, remove the top and sole plates. If the ends of the plates are tied into the sidewalls, cut them off flush. Then use a wrecking bar to pry one end free. Again take care not to damage any floor or ceiling surfaces you want to save. To keep the bar from gouging the surfaces, use a wood block wrapped in cloth behind the head. If you can't pry the plates with this method, cut out several inches in the center of the plate with a wood chisel or reciprocating saw. Use this gap to get beneath the plate with a wrecking bar and pry out both ends.

## Bearing Walls

As with nonbearing walls, begin by stripping the surface material and removing the existing utilities. Removing the finish material doesn't affect the structure of the wall. As long as you don't cut or damage any of the framing, the structural capacity of the wall is intact. Once the framing is exposed, remove all debris from the area.

At this point there are two new factors to consider. One is installing a permanent support beam to carry the load once the wall has been removed. The other is erecting any temporary supports necessary while the work is in progress (see page 42).

To install a permanent beam to replace the bearing wall, you have two options. The first type of beam is a strongback, which is built in the attic and remains out of sight. The existing ceiling joists are suspended from the beam with metal joist hangers. For this installation you need access to the attic area immediately above the

**Removing Nonbearing Walls**

Toenails
Stud
End stud
Sole plate
Cat's paw
Remove the wall covering back to the nearest stud.
Cut sole plate off flush.
Sole plate
Wrecking bar

bearing wall, plus sufficient working space. No temporary supports are necessary because the beam is installed before the wall is torn down.

If there is no attic access, or if there is another story above, you must choose the second option—the exposed beam. This type of beam supports the joists from underneath and is visible in the room. The bottom of the beam should be at least 6 feet 8 inches from the floor to provide sufficient headroom. Temporary supports must be installed before the wall can be torn out.

To install an attic beam, begin by drilling two small holes through the ceiling surface at each end of the bearing wall. From the attic locate the holes and the position of the wall. If there is no subfloor in the attic, put down enough planks or 1/2-inch plywood so you can work safely. If the space between joists is filled with loose insulation, use two long wires to probe through the ceiling holes. If there are insulating batts or blankets in place, pull them back before probing.

Measure the length of wall being demolished. The

### Replacing a Bearing Wall With a Beam

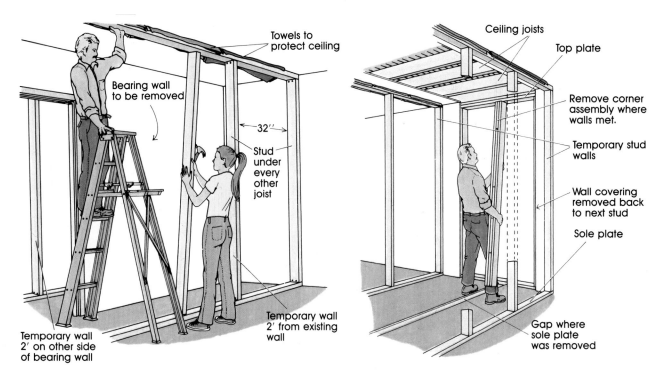

Towels to protect ceiling

Bearing wall to be removed

32″

Stud under every other joist

Temporary wall 2′ from existing wall

Temporary wall 2′ on other side of bearing wall

Ceiling joists

Top plate

Remove corner assembly where walls met.

Temporary stud walls

Wall covering removed back to next stud

Sole plate

Gap where sole plate was removed

proper size of the replacement beam is determined by the length of this span, including bearing points. You can use various span charts for this information, but your best bet is to check the local building code. Call the building department or consult your copy of the code for the correct beam size. Position the ends of the beam so they are directly over studs for carrying the load. You may have to install posts for support.

Generally the new beam must be a 4 by 8, 4 by 10, or 4 by 12. In many instances it doesn't have to be solid lumber. Two pieces of 2-by lumber can be used to fabricate a built-up beam; some codes require three. If you have limited access to the attic and can't get long lengths into the space, build a beam from shorter pieces of 2-by lumber. Nail three widths together with 16d nails staggered every 12 inches or so. Also stagger the joints to achieve the necessary beam length. This is the structural equivalent of solid 4-by lumber.

Position the new beam over the joists and toenail the ends to the outside joists. A 3- to 4-foot 2 by 6 nailed to each end of the beam will distribute its weight along these outside joists. Also be sure there is sufficient bearing under the two outside joists. If the ceiling surface below is lath and plaster, take care not to jar it loose when nailing into the joists. Next nail the beam and the side of each joist together with a metal joist hanger. If two joists overlap beneath the beam, be sure to support both joists with a separate hanger. Once this process is complete, the joists are suspended from the beam and you can remove the wall. Follow the steps outlined earlier for removing a nonbearing wall.

To install a beam within the room, prepare the beam before you build the temporary supports. If the

beam is to be visible, use solid lumber. If you plan to box it with finishing material such as wallboard, you can build up a beam with three widths of 2-by lumber.

The exact length of the beam is difficult to determine until the existing wall is ripped out. If the new beam will run from wall to wall, the length is generally the width of the room, plus the thickness of both finish wall surfaces, plus the width of both side wall studs. Order a beam slightly longer than this. Then once the wall is down, you can take precise measurements and trim the beam to the correct length.

There are several techniques for building temporary supports. Some contractors use adjustable Lally columns, which are like screw jacks except that they include a long length of heavy pipe, or prop the joists with A-shaped supports. The technique outlined here works well using 2-by-4 lumber. The process is similar to building a new partition wall, except that these walls are only temporary.

Because the supports will limit access, place the beam on the floor next to the wall first. If the space is tight getting the beam between the two outer walls, elevate one end of the beam and temporarily secure it. Be sure to protect any finish surfaces from gouging and scarring.

Cut two lengths of 2 by 4 the length of the wall to serve as top and bottom plates. Wider lumber can be used if you have it on hand. Next cut 2-by-4 studs the exact height of the ceiling, less 3 inches (the combined depths of the two plates). If the joists are 16 inches on center, cut enough studs for every other joist. If the joist spacing is wider, cut one stud for each joist.

If the ceiling surface is down, nail the top plate to the joists parallel to the bearing wall and 24 to 30 inches

## Replacing a Bearing Wall With a Beam
### (Continued)

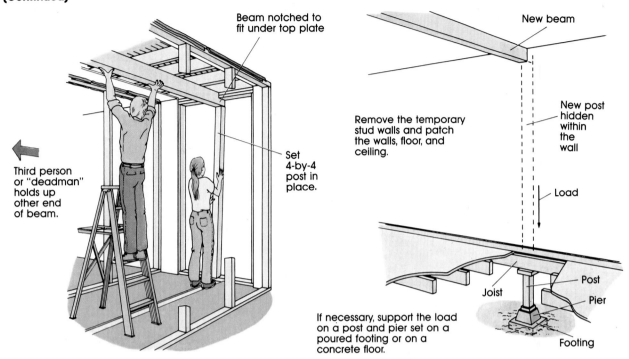

Beam notched to fit under top plate

Set 4-by-4 post in place.

Third person or "deadman" holds up other end of beam.

New beam

Remove the temporary stud walls and patch the walls, floor, and ceiling.

New post hidden within the wall

Load

Joist

Post

Pier

If necessary, support the load on a post and pier set on a poured footing or on a concrete floor.

Footing

away. If the ceiling surface is to be saved, cushion the top plate with a blanket or towels and have a helper hold it in place. Then wedge several studs between the top and sole plate. Position the studs beneath every other joist, beginning with the outside joists. If the studs aren't snug, jam pieces of shim stock underneath to wedge them tight. Toenail the studs to the sole plate, but use double-headed nails or leave the heads exposed for easier removal. Check the position of the studs with a level to be certain they are reasonably vertical.

After this first support is in place, build an identical twin on the opposite side of the wall. One support alone won't do the job. The joists must be shored up on both sides before the wall can be removed. These temporary supports don't have to carry the entire weight of the house. Their purpose is to keep the existing structure from changing shape even slightly. If the ceiling joists are allowed to sag momentarily, you'll have cracked plaster or wallboard to repair.

Once both supports are installed you can remove the wall, following the procedures outlined earlier for nonbearing walls. If the studs seem to be under a lot of pressure when you cut them, or if the ceiling begins to sag, tighten the temporary supports with additional shim stock or add more studs under the unsupported joists. Sometimes you can gauge the pressure before cutting by tapping the studs with a hammer. A solid, ringing sound indicates pressure.

After the studs are out, remove any extra studs in the sidewall that were part of the corner assembly. Cut the wall surfaces back to the nearest stud on either side of the opening. This provides access inside the walls to nail in the beam and posts. (Although you can toenail the

post from the front only in order to minimize patching, this method isn't preferred.)

If the new beam is to be covered, the two top plates can be left in place. Cut off any protruding nails flush with a hacksaw blade. However, the depth of the plates will lower the final height of the beam. If headroom is a problem, remove one or both top plates as explained earlier. Also pull up the sole plate.

Now you can measure and cut the beam to the correct length. You will also need to notch both ends of the beam to fit snugly under the top plates of the sidewalls. If there are two plates of 2-by-4 stock, cut notches 3 inches deep and 3½ inches long at the ends of the beam. Older homes may have only one top plate. Notch accordingly.

Next measure the height from the sole plate to the lower top plate and subtract the depth of the beam. Then cut the posts that will support the beam. The posts can be solid 4 by 4s or built up from two or three 2 by 4s so they are wide enough to support the beam with ⅜-inch plywood spacers between them. With a helper or two, lift the beam in place and wedge the posts beneath it. If some of the ceiling joists are lower than others and interfere, raise them by shimming up the appropriate studs of the temporary bracing. Check the posts with a level to see if they are plumb. If the walls are not exactly plumb, then line up the posts with them. Toenail the posts to the beam and the sole plate. At this point you may need to provide support under the floor for this new post. Once the beam is securely nailed in place and the post is supported, you can remove the temporary supports and patch the openings in the wall and floor. Be sure a metal bracket connects the beam and post.

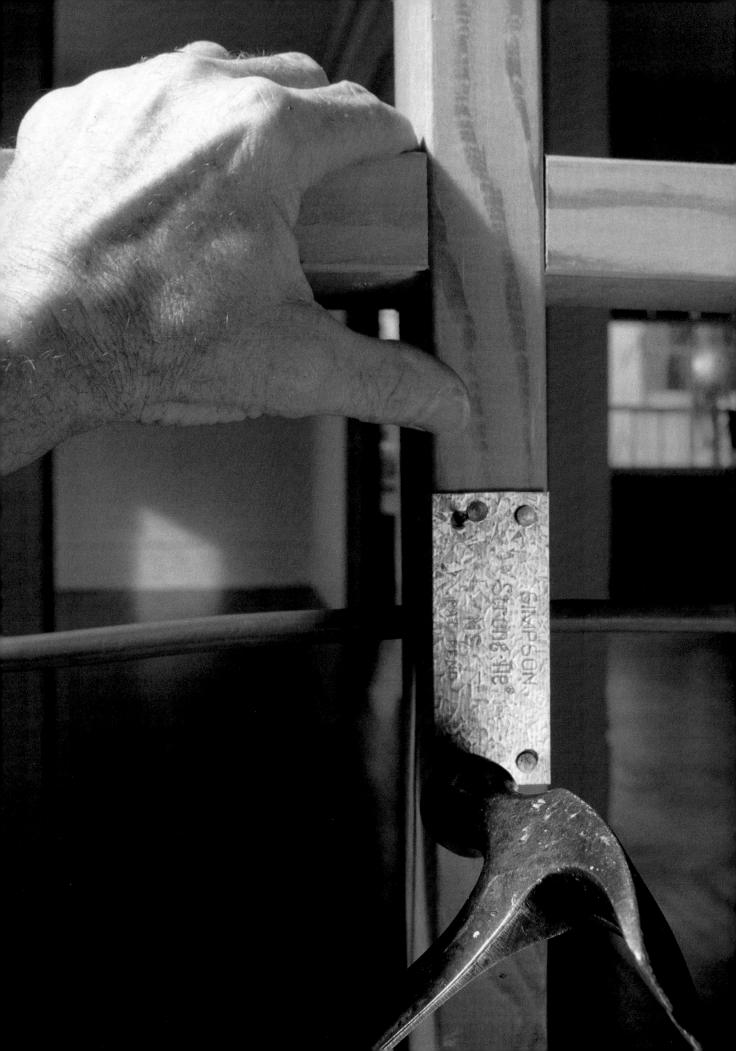

# MAKING INTERIOR CHANGES

Now you can get down to the transformations you've planned and prepared for. Whether you're cutting into walls or building new ones, this chapter will take you through your remodeling projects from start to finish.

In this chapter you will learn step-by-step procedures for five operations common to most interior remodeling projects: making an opening in an existing wall, framing up new partition walls, changing wiring, installing wallboard, and installing insulation.

In addition you will learn how to do three specific projects that have unique problems or approaches: converting an attic to living space, installing a new stairway, and preparing a basement for finishing.

Kitchen and bathroom remodeling are major projects that require their own books, but the basic techniques in this chapter will help you get started.

## Cutting Into an Existing Wall

At times you may want to create a recess in an existing wall. To install a prebuilt cabinet, such as a medicine chest or ironing board, or to build in-wall storage for books, towels, or collectibles, follow these procedures.

The first step is to determine the optimum size for the opening. Begin by checking the location of the studs (see page 31). If the studs are conventionally spaced 16 inches on center, the space between them is roughly 14 1/2 inches. If you cut one stud, the opening is increased to 30 1/2 inches. The depth available depends on the finish wall surface and stud width. With wallboard this is usually about 4 inches; with lath and plaster the depth ranges from 4 to 5 inches. If you need more depth, use a wider jamb and build out into the room several inches.

Next examine the wall for utility systems that may be hidden inside (see page 39). If you can, move the location to either side to avoid unnecessary rerouting. Reconsider the exact width and location once you've located the studs and utilities. If these two factors aren't limiting, choose the size and location that require the

*Remodeling projects may require rerouting wires or cables or installing protective metal plates as shown here.*

least amount of work to produce the desired result. Perhaps the opening should be smaller or larger than planned originally.

**Cutting an opening between studs.** Use a framing square and mark the outline on the wall with a pencil. Check the lines with a level or plumb bob, since the ceiling and floor may not be absolutely level. Drill two starter holes at the opposite corners; then cut out the opening with a drywall saw. Keep the blade shallow so the surface on the opposite side isn't damaged. The opening will expose the hidden side of the opposite wall. Blobs of dried plaster that has oozed between the lath, called *plaster keys,* may intrude into the space. If they are especially thick, chip them off carefully with a chisel.

With some installations, such as an ironing board or a niche to be surfaced with new wallboard, you should add a 2-by-4 header and sill to the opening. To support the header and sill during nailing, first nail small blocks of 1 by 2s or 2 by 4s to the studs or drive in several guide nails. Then rest the header and sill on these supports and toenail to the studs.

If the unit is a prebuilt cabinet such as a medicine chest, you can generally dispense with the header and sill. Simply insert the cabinet into the opening and attach to the studs with nails or wood screws through the sides.

If you are building your own cabinet, it's best to assemble it first, complete with back and sides. Build it at a workbench and then install it like a prebuilt. Because the studs may not be square, make the unit slightly smaller than the rough opening and shim as necessary. If you use 1/2-inch plywood or 1-inch wood for the top and bottom, the header and sill aren't necessary. To protect the opposite wall surface, and yet minimize the unit's depth, use 3/16-inch plywood for the back. Also leave a gap of 1/8 inch between the unit and the opposite wall.

**Cutting an opening through studs.** First determine if the wall is bearing or nonbearing (see page 30). If the wall is nonbearing, mark the opening 1 1/2 inches higher

### Cutting a Recess in a Wall

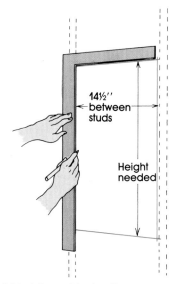

**14½"** between studs

Height needed

1. Mark the cabinet outline on the wall.

Starter hole

Starter hole

2. Use a wallboard saw to cut out the opening.

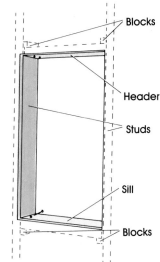

Blocks

Header

Studs

Sill

Blocks

3. Nail small blocks to the studs where top of header and bottom of sill are to be.

4. Hold header and sill against the blocks and toenail to the studs.

### Cabinet Built Out From a Recess

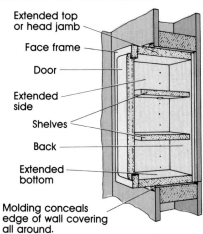

Extended top or head jamb

Face frame

Door

Extended side

Shelves

Back

Extended bottom

Molding conceals edge of wall covering all around.

### Installing a Prebuilt Cabinet

Secure cabinet with finish nails or screws through sides into studs.

Medicine cabinet

Completed opening

### Gypsum Lath and Plaster

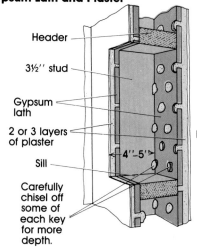

Header

3½" stud

Gypsum lath

2 or 3 layers of plaster

Sill

Carefully chisel off some of each key for more depth.

4"–5"

### Wood Lath and Plaster

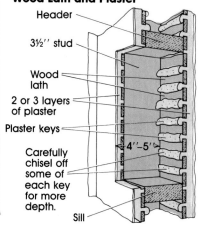

Header

3½" stud

Wood lath

2 or 3 layers of plaster

Plaster keys

Carefully chisel off some of each key for more depth.

4"–5"

Sill

### Gypsum Wallboard

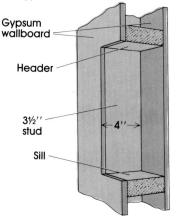

Gypsum wallboard

Header

3½" stud

Sill

4"

and lower than the size of the finish opening. This allows room to cut the studs and install a 2-by-4 header and sill. Ideally the width of the opening corresponds exactly to the width between existing studs. This minimizes patching the wall. But even if the width doesn't correspond, cut back to the outer studs to gain access for nailing.

Once the wall surface is removed, mark the exposed studs with a square and cut with a saw. Since the opposite wall surface is still nailed to the studs, sawing and removing the pieces can be a problem. To minimize damage, rock the cut studs with your hands or use a hammer to knock them sideways. Take care not to puncture the opposite surface. Once the studs are out, install the header and sill by nailing through them into the cut ends of the studs above and below. Also toenail them to the full-length studs on either side. If you need to narrow the opening, toenail a pair of 2-by-4 cripple studs between the header and sill to frame a smaller rough opening. Or you can end nail the cripples before installing the header and sill.

If the wall is bearing, before you can cut the studs you must build temporary supports on either side of the wall (see page 42). Then after the studs are cut, you must install a header large enough to carry the load. If the opening is less than 4 feet wide, a header of 4-by-4 lumber or two 2 by 4s set on edge can generally be used. The latter may be easier to install, since they can be toenailed in separately. Use $3/8$-inch plywood spacers between the 2 by 4s to build the width to just less than $3 1/2$ inches. If the opening is 4 to 5 feet wide, the header should be a 4 by 6. Check your local code to determine the exact specifications.

Mark the wall surface as described previously. In this case the opening must be large enough to accommodate the increased header size. Cut and strip the wall surface; then erect temporary supports on both sides of the wall. The supports should be the width of the opening, plus one joist on either side.

Next cut and remove the portions of the studs inside the opening. Insert two trimmer studs inside the wall cavity and nail them to the full studs on either side. Position the header over the trimmer studs and toenail it in place. Then face nail a 2-by-4 sill to the cut studs below and toenail to the trimmer studs on either side. If you need to narrow the opening, toenail 2-by-4 cripple studs between the header and sill. Once the rough framing is complete, the temporary supports can be removed.

### Building a Pass-Through

To create a pass-through between two rooms, follow the general guidelines for building a recess within a wall. There are some differences, however. Obviously you will remove both sides of the wall instead of just one. But you need extra access on only one side to install the header. As a result the second side can be cut after the header is installed. And because it can be cut to the exact size, you won't have to patch the wall.

A second consideration is building some type of countertop. The 2-by-4 rough sill is strong enough to support a narrow countertop, which can be a 1-inch finish board up to 10 inches wide. Moldings underneath either side of this finish piece will provide additional support.

Finally, while a pass-through can be convenient, sometimes it's desirable to close off rooms, so plan to install folding door or shutters to cover the opening.

### Building a Pass-Through

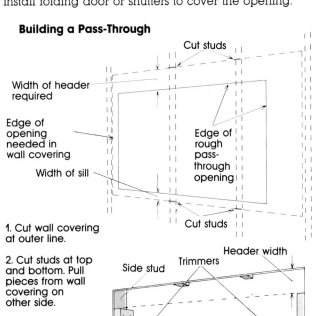

1. Cut wall covering at outer line.

2. Cut studs at top and bottom. Pull pieces from wall covering on other side.

3. Install sill. Face nail to cut studs; toenail to side studs.

4. Install trimmers the height of the rough opening and nail to side studs.

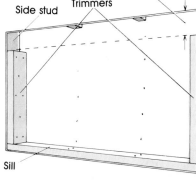

5. Install header on top of the trimmers; toenail it in place.

6. Install cripple studs as needed.

7. Cut wall covering on other side to edge of rough opening.

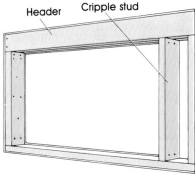

8. Patch around rough opening with wallboard scraps. Cover joints, nail dimples with compound.

9. Cut and install head and side jambs.

10. Cut and install countertop.

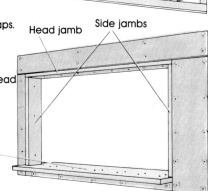

## Adding a New Doorway

Cutting into an existing wall to create a new doorway is essentially the same as building a pass-through or in-wall storage. One difference is that the rough opening extends to the floor. Another is the problem of hanging the door once the framing is complete. Using a prehung door solves this nicely.

Most rooms have 32-inch doors, but a range of widths from 24 to 36 inches is possible. The standard door height is 6 feet 8 inches, but this can vary as well. For walls finished with wallboard, 4$\frac{5}{8}$ inches is the standard jamb size. For lath and plaster walls, the jamb size ranges from 5$\frac{1}{8}$ to 5$\frac{3}{8}$ inches.

The size of the opening depends on the width of the frame and the location of the studs. As a rule the smallest width possible is the width of the finish frame plus 4 inches. This allows one trimmer stud on either side of the opening plus an extra $\frac{1}{2}$ inch on both sides. This $\frac{1}{2}$-inch clearance is necessary because the existing studs may not be perfectly vertical.

The height of the opening should be the height of the prehung frame, plus the depth of the header, plus $\frac{1}{2}$-inch clearance. If the wall is nonbearing, the header can be two 2 by 4s laid flat. One is sufficient, but two minimize the flex in the wall and lessen the chance of cracked plaster or wallboard when the door is slammed shut. Laying the headers flat simplifies the nailing, since they can be face nailed to the cripple studs overhead.

If the wall is bearing, the header generally should be the equivalent of 4-by-4 lumber. But again, check your local code for the proper size.

Once the dimensions of the opening are established, follow the procedures for cutting in-wall storage (see page 45). If the wall is bearing, be sure to provide temporary supports before you cut the studs. Frame the opening as shown in the sketch below. Before nailing, check the position of the trimmer studs and header with a level or plumb bob to be sure the opening is square.

After the rough frame is complete, cut out the sole plate with a hand saw or reciprocating saw. Since the bottom of the sole plate is on the subfloor, you'll need a chisel to cut all the way through. Protect the finish floor by taping down scraps of cardboard. Patch the opening between the floors with a hardwood threshold or a filler

**Adding a New Doorway**

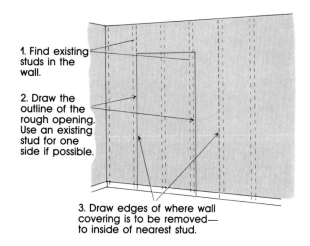

1. Find existing studs in the wall.

2. Draw the outline of the rough opening. Use an existing stud for one side if possible.

3. Draw edges of where wall covering is to be removed—to inside of nearest stud.

4. Remove baseboard and any other trim. Cut wall covering from marked area on one side of the wall.

5. Remove studs within the area.

6. Install new framing: studs, trimmers, header, and cripples.

7. Cut out sole plate in doorway and fill the resulting gap in the finished floor with suitable material.

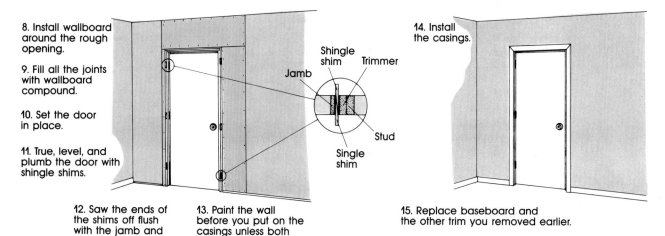

8. Install wallboard around the rough opening.

9. Fill all the joints with wallboard compound.

10. Set the door in place.

11. True, level, and plumb the door with shingle shims.

12. Saw the ends of the shims off flush with the jamb and wall surfaces.

13. Paint the wall before you put on the casings unless both wall and casings are to be the same color.

Shingle shim
Trimmer
Jamb
Stud
Single shim

14. Install the casings.

15. Replace baseboard and the other trim you removed earlier.

board that can be covered later with finish flooring. You should also install wallboard around the rough opening before you install the door and frame. (For wallboard instructions, see page 55.)

After the wallboard is finished, you're ready to hang the door and frame. Handling and positioning the frame are usually easier if the door is removed first, but this is a matter of preference. If you feel you can manipulate the door and frame as a unit, fine. Otherwise tap out the hinge pins and set the door aside. If you prefer to hide all the finish nails behind the doorstop, remove it. If not leave the stop in place and face nail through the jambs.

Cut off any protective ends on the frame and slip the frame into the rough opening. Begin shimming between the jamb and trimmer stud at the lower hinge. Once you have the approximate position, drive a finishing nail through the jamb and shims into the trimmer. Continue the process all around the frame, checking repeatedly with your level to be sure the frame is plumb. Also check the width of the frame to be sure it remains constant. Otherwise the door won't swing freely. Make sure the jamb is centered in the opening and extends flush with the finish wall surface on either side. Once the frame is securely shimmed and nailed, cut the shims flush with the edge of the jambs. Use a hand saw or score the edges of the shims with a utility knife and break them with a hammer. Reinstall the door and stop if they've been removed, and trim out the frame with casings.

The process of building a new partition wall can be simple or complex, depending primarily on where the wall is positioned. If the wall runs perpendicular to the existing ceiling joists, it's easier to install than if it runs parallel. And if the new wall runs both parallel to and between two joists, the job may involve cutting into the ceiling and wall surfaces to add blocking.

The first step in building a new wall is to determine its proper location. If the wall runs perpendicular to the ceiling joists, nailing through the finish surface to the joists is no problem. If the wall runs parallel to the joists, locate it directly beneath a joist whenever possible.

### Attaching Walls

If the wall must run parallel and between the joists, install nailing blocks to secure the wall to the ceiling. If you have access to the attic above the room, nail in short lengths of 2 by 4s between the two joists. Space the blocks 32 inches apart if possible (48 inches is all right).

If you don't have access above the room, there are several alternative methods for securing the wall to the ceiling. One is to drill through the top plate and finish ceiling and use toggle bolts to connect the two. Space these about every 24 inches. This method isn't recommended for walls that include a door.

A second technique requires stripping away the ceiling surface between the joists and toenailing the blocks in position. This method is practical only if the

### Attaching Partition Walls to the Ceiling

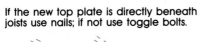

If the new top plate is directly beneath joists use nails; if not use toggle bolts.

1. Remove the bolt from the toggle, put a large washer on the bolt, and screw it back on the toggle.

2. Drill a hole through the top plate and ceiling large enough to accept the toggle. Fold the toggle, insert it through the hole, and let it snap open above the ceiling.

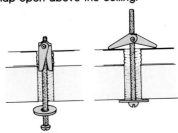

3. Tighten the screw to pull the toggle against the upper surface of the ceiling covering.

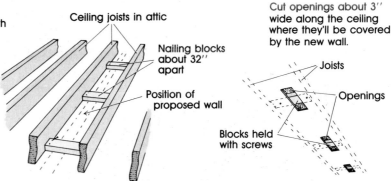

Ceiling joists in attic

Nailing blocks about 32" apart

Position of proposed wall

Install nailing blocks between joists in the attic from above or strip the ceiling and put them in from below.

Cut openings about 3" wide along the ceiling where they'll be covered by the new wall.

Joists

Openings

Blocks held with screws

Cut 2-by-4 blocks about 13½" long, insert them through the openings, turn them perpendicular to the joists, and hold them in place with flat-head screws.

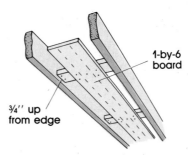

1-by-6 board

¾" up from edge

Nail the top plate of the new wall to the middle of the 1 by 6, leaving a nailing surface for ceiling covering on each side.

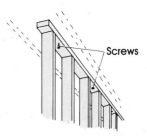

Screws

Screw the top plate of the new wall to the blocks.

ceiling is to be removed anyway. With the ceiling sur-face down, you will need to provide a nailing surface for applying wallboard. This can be achieved by nailing a 1 by 2 or 2 by 4 along the edge of the joist, or by setting the nailing blocks back ¾ inch and inserting a 1-by-6 board above the top plate (see the sketches for details).

A third technique involves slightly less work but does not create as strong a connection. Cut several channels through the ceiling surface where the new wall will be positioned. Each should measure 3 inches wide and 13½ inches long. Space the openings 32 inches apart. Insert a 2-by-4 block 13½ inches long (or 1 inch shorter than the space between joists) and turn it 90 degrees so it's perpendicular to the joists. (If you insert the block end-first, the opening can be smaller.) Hold the block with one hand, and drive two wallboard or wood screws through the ceiling into the ends of the block. Then use wood screws to attach the top plate to the blocks. The width of the new wall will cover the channels—only the screw holes in the ceiling surface need to be patched.

After attaching the ceiling blocks, locate the existing studs in the sidewalls. The new wall must be nailed to a stud or blocks installed between studs. Two blocks for each end of an 8-foot wall are generally sufficient. Toggle bolts can also be used.

## Framing Walls

Interior partition walls are normally framed with 2-by-4 lumber. To frame a bathroom wet wall, you may need to use 2-by-6 studs to accommodate the size of the drain-waste-vent lines. Begin by measuring the length of the new wall. Because the walls and ceilings in an older home may not be square, measure along the floor and ceiling. Also be sure either to remove baseboard and

ceiling moldings beforehand or chisel out an opening wide enough for the new wall.

Next cut two 2 by 4s to serve as top and sole plates. For a nonbearing wall, a single top plate is sufficient. Lay the two plates side by side and mark off the location for the studs and any door openings. Although some codes allow 24-inch spacing for nonbearing walls, the pre-ferred spacing for all partition walls is 16 inches on center. Use a square and pencil to indicate the location of each stud. If the position of the last stud at the end of the plate is less than 16 inches, fine. Don't change the layout to make the studs come out even.

Nor should you change the spacing for a doorway. Once you see the layout on the plates, however, you may decide to move the door location slightly to take advan-tage of the normal stud spacing. (For information on framing a door opening, see page 48.) Because you are building a completely new wall and can guarantee the rough door opening will be square, allow ¼-inch in-stead of ½-inch clearance on each side. To simplify cut-ting out the opening when the sole plate is nailed to the floor, turn the sole plate over and cut through half its depth at the door location.

At two points along the ceiling, mark the location of the edge of the top plate and snap a chalk line. Use a plumb bob to mark the position of the sole plate directly beneath the top plate and snap a second chalk line. Nail the sole plate to the floor with 10d nails every 16 inches. As a precaution, check in the basement first to be certain you won't puncture any plumbing or heating pipes. Don't nail between any door opening. If the floor is badly warped or uneven, shim the low spots beneath the plate.

Make several measurements between the ceiling and floor. Be sure the measurements take into account

### Framing and Attaching Stud Walls

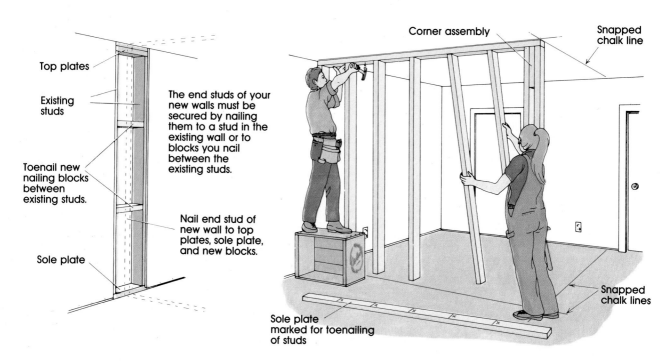

Top plates

Existing studs

Toenail new nailing blocks between existing studs.

Sole plate

The end studs of your new walls must be secured by nailing them to a stud in the existing wall or to blocks you nail between the existing studs.

Nail end stud of new wall to top plates, sole plate, and new blocks.

Corner assembly

Snapped chalk line

Snapped chalk lines

Sole plate marked for toenailing of studs

the top plate. It is easiest to temporarily lay the top plate on top of the sole plate while making the measurements. If the floor-to-ceiling height varies more than ⅛ inch, measure and cut each stud separately. If the dimensions vary only slightly, cut all studs to the same length.

Next lay the top plate on edge and nail into the end of each stud with two 16d nails. If a doorway is included, nail in the trimmer studs, header, and cripple studs. With a helper, raise the entire framework with the studs dangling beneath, position the top plate along the chalk line, and nail to the ceiling joists or blocks with 10d or 16d nails. The size of the nail depends on the ceiling surface, but nail into the joist at least 1 inch. If necessary, use shim stock to fill any gaps. Use a plumb bob to guarantee that the new wall is plumb. Once the top plate is secured, attach the two end studs to the sidewall framing with 10d nails. Then toenail all other studs to the sole plate, first checking each stud for plumb.

Short sections of 2 by 4s nailed between the studs may be required as fireblocking. Check your local code: the blocks may not be required. They take time to install, but add rigidity to the wall and provide an additional nailing surface for wallboard and paneling.

If you are erecting two or more walls that intersect at right angles, reinforce the corner assemblies. This is necessary for greater strength and to provide a nailing surface for applying wallboard and paneling. The easiest technique is to use two full studs with three short 2-by-4 blocks nailed in between them. Full-length studs can also be used. (See the sketches for corner assemblies.)

**An alternative technique.** If the ceiling or sidewalls are badly warped or not square, or if there is no room to lift up a built wall, your best bet is to nail in the top and sole plates first. Then measure, cut, and toenail each stud

separately. This approach also works well if you have no one to help lift the framework in place. The only real difference is toenailing the studs both top and bottom, rather than end nailing to the top plate first.

**A second alternative.** If you have sufficient floor space and a helper to assist with lifting, you may be able to frame the wall completely on the floor and then stand it up. But first determine if the walls and ceiling are square. (If they are not, use the first technique described.) This technique generally works best with shorter wall sections that don't extend the entire width of the room. Otherwise you'll have trouble getting the wall in position without jamming the ceiling and sidewalls. If you do decide to use this technique, cut the studs 3¼ inches less than the height from floor to ceiling. This allows for the thickness of two plates plus ¼ inch for clearance. Once the wall is raised in place, wedge shim stock between the top plate and the ceiling. Then nail the top plate to the joists and the sole plate to the floor.

## Wiring New Receptacles

After the wall is framed and nailed in place, rough in any electrical systems involved. If the local code requires this work to be done by a licensed professional, now is the time for the electrician to arrive. If you're able to handle the work yourself, be sure to secure the appropriate permits before you begin.

In many cases all that's necessary is one or more electrical outlets. This section describes how to extend an existing electrical circuit to provide outlets for a new partition wall. It is not within the scope of this book, however, to provide a complete discussion on all aspects of wiring. If your project requires more detailed information, consult Ortho's book *Basic Wiring Techniques*.

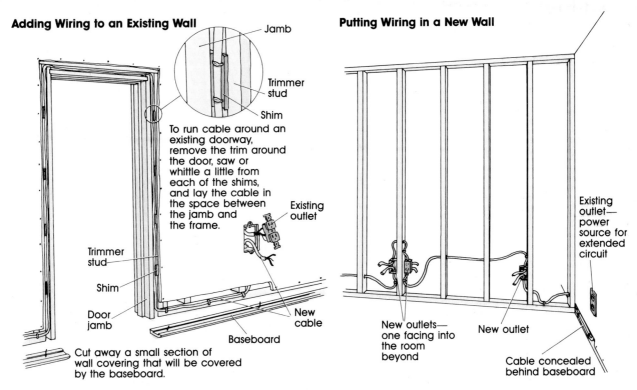

**Adding Wiring to an Existing Wall**

Jamb

Trimmer stud

Shim

To run cable around an existing doorway, remove the trim around the door, saw or whittle a little from each of the shims, and lay the cable in the space between the jamb and the frame.

Existing outlet

Trimmer stud

Shim

Door jamb

New cable

Baseboard

Cut away a small section of wall covering that will be covered by the baseboard.

**Putting Wiring in a New Wall**

Existing outlet—power source for extended circuit

New outlets—one facing into the room beyond

New outlet

Cable concealed behind baseboard

**Extending an existing circuit.** The following summary covers the steps in adding outlets and switches to a new wall. The purpose here is to help you see what's involved so you can relate the wiring process to other remodeling operations.

First determine where new outlets should go. Electrical codes generally specify the approximate location of new outlets and switches. For example:

■ Any wall more than 2 feet in length should have at least one outlet.

■ No point along a new wall should be more than 6 feet from an outlet.

■ Outlets should be 12 to 18 inches above the floor.

■ Although not specified by code, it's common for lighting circuits to have 10 to 12 outlets and for small-appliance circuits to have 6.

■ Switches should be 48 inches from the floor and on the latch side of a doorway, as well as at each entrance to a room and at both ends of hallways and stairs.

Your next step is to find a source of power to tap into. For one or two new outlets, this usually means the closest outlet, junction box, or source-fed switch of an existing circuit. For larger extensions, it may mean running back to the breaker panel. Avoid these sources:

■ A single-appliance circuit. Whether 120 or 240 volts, it is intended to serve only one fixed appliance, such as a dishwasher or furnace motor.

■ A switch at the end of a loop or in the middle of a three-way switch loop.

■ A junction box with wiring from several circuits.

■ A potentially overloaded circuit. You can calculate the future electrical demand by adding up the total watts anticipated and dividing by 120 volts. The quotient, the number of amps potentially demanded by the circuit, should not exceed the rating of the circuit breaker (usually 15 amps).

Once a source is located, plan the most accessible route for running cable to the new outlets and back to the source. Possibilities for routing the cable include:

■ Behind baseboards, either in existing gaps or notches cut into the lath and plaster.

■ Under the floor, as long as there is a crawl space.

■ In an accessible attic.

■ Around a doorway in a groove behind the casings.

Most routes will involve fishing wires through walls or floors at some point, but do choose the path with the easiest access.

**Installing the system.** First install outlet and switch boxes in the new wall. Mount them with the front edge extended 1/2 inch beyond the studs so the edge will be flush with the final finish wall.

Then run new cable between the boxes and back to the source, drilling through studs, sole plates, or top plates where necessary. Be sure to staple the cable every 4 feet and within 12 inches of metal boxes and 8 inches of plastic boxes. Leave 8 to 10 inches of cable within each box.

Before running cable into the final source, which is usually an outlet or junction box, turn off the electrical circuit. Then run cable into the old box through an unused knockout hole. Leave 8 to 10 inches of cable for connecting to the old receptacle. Before turning on the circuit again, install all new receptacles and fixtures and connect the new run to the existing power source. Restore power and double check your work with a voltage tester and polarity tester.

### Running Cable Under the House

### Running the Cable Through the Attic

### Running the Cable Under the Floor

Drill a ¾'' hole 2½–3'' inside a pilot hole (drilled from above).

Push the cable up through the hole. A helper can pull it through the box.

Run the cable through a hole in the top plate above the new box and down to the new box.

### Running Cable in the Attic

Cable

Joists

Studs

Cable

Guard strips

Joists

Studs

# ADDING INSULATION

Unless you live in a mild climate, a number of the projects in this book require adding insulation. An attic or garage converted to living space, for example, should be adequately insulated once the framing is complete and before the walls and ceilings are finished. As long as the studs and joists are exposed this is an easy job to do yourself.

## Choosing Materials

Insulation is available in several different forms. The chart on the next page compares blankets, batts, loose and blown fill, and rigid panels.

Insulating materials are rated according to their resistance to heat flow, expressed in an R-value. The higher the number, the greater the insulating value. For example, 3½ inches of fiberglass is rated R-11; 6 inches is rated R-19. The rating varies not only with the thickness of the material but also with the type.

The right R-value for the job depends on:

■ *The climate.* The weather in Miami is obviously different from the weather in Minneapolis, and so are the recommended R-values for insulation.

■ *The surface to be insulated.* R-value requirements differ for walls, ceilings, and floors.

■ *The local building code.* As a result of the energy crisis in the late seventies, a number of states and counties have adopted rigorous energy-saving standards for new construction and remodeling.

To find the proper R-value for your project, check with the building department. In some situations compliance with the code is mandatory; in other cases the standards are intended as guidelines and compliance is optional. Research the requirements thoroughly before you begin.

Along with the insulation, you should plan to install some type of vapor barrier. The interior of the average house contains a tremendous amount of moisture. If warm, moist air from the inside of the house meets cool air from the outside, condensation results. Condensation within the exterior walls of your house can create a number of problems, ranging from a fungus called dry rot to paint that perennially flakes and peels. Excess moisture can also cause some types of insulation to compact, which lessens their effectiveness.

Installing a water-resistant vapor barrier combats this problem. Asphalt-impregnated kraft paper or aluminum foil often faces one side of the insulation. Or you can add the barrier separately in thin plastic sheets.

## Types of Insulation

| Form | R-Value* | Materials | Principal Use | Installation Method | Comments |
|---|---|---|---|---|---|
| **Blankets or Batts** | 3.7 3.3 | Rock wool Glass fiber | Walls Floors Ceilings Attics Roofs | Fitted between wood frame studs, joists, and beams | Most common form do-it-yourselfers use; suited for standard stud and joist spacing without obstructions; batts easier to handle |
| **Loose or Blown Fill** | 2.9 2.2 3.6 2.4 2.7 | Rock wool Glass fiber Cellulose fiber Vermiculite Perlite | Floors Walls Hard-to-reach places Finished areas | Poured between joists or blown into place with special equipment | Easy to use in irregularly shaped areas; blown fill, the only option for finished areas, should be installed by a professional |
| **Rigid Panels** | 4.0 5.0 7.4 4.5 | Molded polystyrene Extruded polystyrene Isocyanurate board Fiberglass board | Unfinished walls Basement masonry walls Exterior surfaces | Cut to fit and secured in place; must be covered with finishing material for fire safety | High insulating value for relatively little thickness; plastic boards are highly flammable |

*Brookhaven National Laboratories

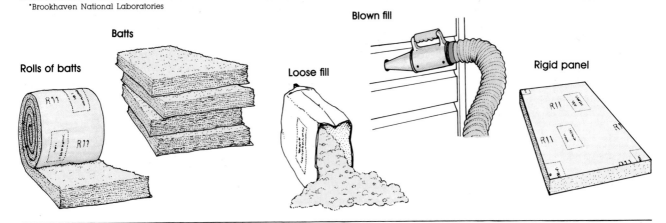

Rolls of batts  Batts  Loose fill  Blown fill  Rigid panel

### Installing a Vapor Barrier

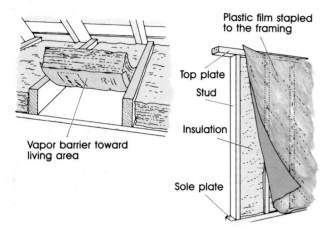

Plastic film stapled to the framing

Top plate

Stud

Insulation

Sole plate

Vapor barrier toward living area

The cardinal rule to remember is that the vapor barrier always goes toward the warm or heated side of the house, that is, toward the inside. This means that in an attic ceiling the vapor barrier faces down, along the exterior wall it faces in, and between the basement floor joists it faces up. It's essential to heed this simple rule—otherwise you'll only make the moisture problem worse.

### Installing Insulation

You should follow a number of safety precautions when installing insulation.

■ *Dress appropriately.* Minute particles of insulation can be irritating to the skin and lungs, so protect yourself. This means wearing long sleeves, gloves, and a hat. Goggles and a respirator are extremely important. After the job is done, take a shower right away and launder your work clothes.

■ *Keep insulation at least 3 inches away from hot objects.* Install a sheet metal baffle around problem areas such as recessed light fixtures, chimneys, and flues to minimize the danger of fires.

■ *Don't block any vents or ducts.* This is especially true in attic spaces where good ventilation is needed to prevent condensation buildup. If the attic floor is being insulated, make sure there are eave vents, gable vents, or roof vents to provide air circulation. For rafter installations allow at least 2 inches between the insulation and the roof sheathing so air can circulate freely from the eaves to the ridge of the roof.

■ *Keep aluminum foil vapor barriers away from knob and tube wiring.* As the fabric insulation on this older wiring ages and begins to fray, the aluminum could cause a short circuit.

**Blankets and batts.** To cut through blankets and batts, place the insulation on a stable cutting surface. A wide piece of plywood or wallboard on the floor is best. With the vapor barrier toward you, compress the insulation with a scrap piece of wood as a straightedge. Make the cut with a sharp utility knife. As a rule, pieces should be cut an extra inch long so the insulation will fill the space.

Push the insulation into the cavity between the studs or joists. It's more efficient to cut and place several pieces

and then secure them. Spread the flanges of the vapor barrier and staple every 6 inches or so along the edge of the stud or joist. Use a $3/8$-inch heavy-duty staple gun. Set the insulation back from the face of the wood to create a $3/4$-inch dead air pocket between the insulation and the finish wall. Don't compress the insulation tightly because its R-value depends on its thickness.

An alternate technique is to overlap the flanges on the face of the stud and then staple. This technique creates a better seal but can interfere with the application of the finish surface, such as wallboard. It also eliminates the desirable dead air space between insulation and finish wall. Make sure the flanges and staples lie flat against the studs.

When you install insulation from under the house, the stapling flanges will be out of reach because the facing goes toward the floor. To hold the blankets in place, staple wire, nylon string, or chicken wire across the bottom of the joists or wedge spring clips between them.

Whenever possible insulation should be placed behind the plumbing lines. It may be necessary to split the insulation and run some front and back. If the insulation fits easily behind the wiring, fine. If this creates a problem or requires too much compression, cover the wiring.

Fill any small openings by cutting scrap pieces to fit. Any rips or tears should be patched with duct tape. For the best possible job, joints between batts should be taped as well.

If the insulation is unfaced, you must add a vapor barrier. The insulation is generally wide enough to stay in place once it's pressed snugly between the studs or joists. After the wall or ceiling spaces are filled, cover the entire surface with a thin sheet of plastic. This can be 2-mil polyethylene, but 4-mil is easier to use and tears less frequently. Start at the top and work down, stapling to the wood as you go. Keep the surface taut and the staples flat because a finish material must be added later. Seal any seams or tears with tape. Some contractors recommend this technique even if the batts or blankets are faced with a vapor barrier. It's faster than patching the joints and cuts and results in a superior seal.

**Rigid panels.** Rigid panels are cut with a utility knife or saw. Follow the manufacturer's recommendations for proper installation. Some panels are secured with mastic applied to the back. If the panels are used for an exposed beam ceiling, quarter round molding around the edges can hold them in place. Pressed fiberglass panels are available with a prefinished vinyl surface. Other materials such as polystyrene are flammable and must be covered with a fire-resistant material such as $1/2$-inch wallboard.

**Loose fill.** First be sure any vents or flues are safely baffled. Next you will need to add a vapor barrier. Cut strips of 4-mil plastic wide enough to fit between the joists with enough extra to lap up the sides several inches. Smooth the plastic in place and staple to the sides of the joists. Repair any cuts or holes with tape. Then pour in the insulation between the joists to the proper thickness. Keep the fill loose and fluffy, not packed down.

# INSTALLING WALLBOARD

Wallboard is known by many names. Whether it's called gypsumboard, plasterboard, drywall, or Sheetrock (a trade name), the product is the same: a solid gypsum core covered on both sides with heavy paper. It's an inexpensive, all-purpose surface that can be used in any room of the house.

Installing wallboard panels is relatively simple. It's the taping and finishing that require patience and practice. Before you decide to do it yourself, consider hiring professionals to handle the job. This is especially true if you dislike projects requiring careful attention to detail. As a rule of thumb, if more than three panels or 100 square feet are involved, get estimates first. The total cost of a professional job may compare favorably with your material costs alone.

## Planning

Begin by planning the installation on paper. Work out a pattern that results in the fewest number of joints. Although minimizing waste is always a concern, in this case minimizing your labor is even more important. Wallboard is so inexpensive that you should use full sheets whenever you can. It's not worth bothering with small pieces just to save a few dollars.

The long edges of wallboard panels are tapered slightly to accommodate several coats of joint compound; the 4-foot edges are not. So plan to join panels along the long, beveled edge whenever possible. When end joints can't be avoided, stagger them so they'll be less noticeable.

Longer panels, such as 4 by 12s or even 4 by 16s, make it possible to span the entire length of most walls. Planning joints to fall above and below windows and above doors also means less taping. For ceilings, use panels that span the longest distance, providing they run perpendicular to the joists. The longer lengths are heavier and harder to install, but you'll save time because less finishing is required.

## Preparing Studs and Joists

Before any panels are applied, prepare the studs and joists. Pull any nails and scrape away small pieces of old wallboard or paneling. If you are replacing lath and plaster, the new wallboard probably isn't the same thickness as the old surface. In order to make the trim around doors and windows lie properly, use any of the following techniques that apply.

■ Add matching wood strips behind the trim to fill the gaps. This takes time but is practical if there isn't much trim. If the gaps are small, you may be able to fill them with caulking after the wallboard is installed.

■ Use two layers of wallboard. This solution is generally too expensive to be feasible, although it does provide extra soundproofing.

■ Shim the studs with old lath or any suitable stock that creates the proper depth. For example, to replace

**Installing Wallboard**

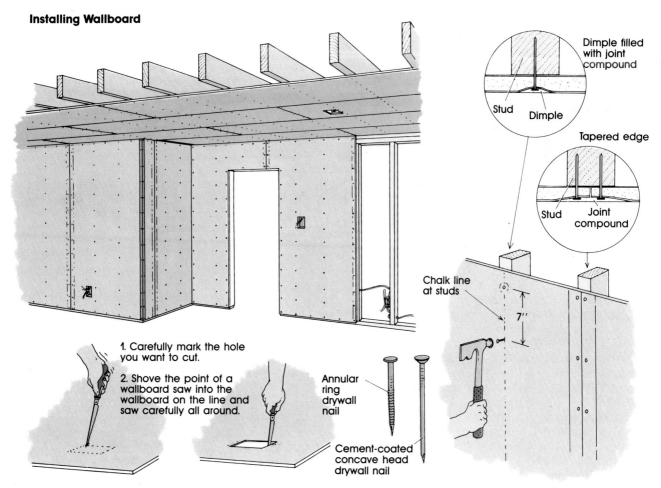

1. Carefully mark the hole you want to cut.

2. Shove the point of a wallboard saw into the wallboard on the line and saw carefully all around.

Annular ring drywall nail

Cement-coated concave head drywall nail

Dimple filled with joint compound

Stud    Dimple

Tapered edge

Stud    Joint compound

Chalk line at studs

7"

3/4-inch plaster with 1/2-inch wallboard, shim the studs with 1/4- by 1 1/2-inch lath. Tack the lath in place along the length of each stud. When the panels are applied, use a longer nail that drives through both wallboard and lath into the stud.

■ Check the studs with a plumb bob to see if they are reasonably plumb. As long as the wall is a smooth plane, slight irregularities won't be noticed. Use shim stock to correct obvious problems.

■ Check the wall and ceiling surfaces to see if they are square. Measure the diagonals of the surface. If the dimensions disagree by more than 1/2 inch, you may need to trim one or more panels along the edge to fit. Or you can try compensating slightly as each panel goes up. Otherwise you'll come to a panel that falls off the edge of a stud or joist.

■ Check the wall and ceiling for sufficient nailing surfaces. Wallboard panels should not be applied with unsupported edges. If a corner or ceiling line needs a nailing surface, nail in lengths of 1 by 2s or 2 by 4s as needed. If only part of the surface is to be replaced, and the old wallboard is cut next to a stud, nail a 1 by 2 along the stud to serve as a nailer for the new panel.

■ Check where any wires or pipes go through the studs or joists. They should be at least 1 1/4 inches back from the edge, or protected by metal stud guards.

■ Finally evaluate whether any of the walls needs additional shear strength. Adding shear strength usually involves glue nailing 1/4-inch or 3/8-inch plywood to the studs before wallboard is applied. Your building department or a qualified engineer can advise you and recommend a nailing pattern for the plywood panels. If you have to strip some walls anyway, adding shear panels in the right places is a very cheap way to substantially strengthen your home.

## Cutting Panels

When cutting panels, use a guide such as a 4-foot-long wallboard T-square or a straightedge. Any long, straight piece of wood will do. The panel can be leaning against the wall or lying flat on the floor. With a sharp utility knife, cut through the face paper and score the gypsum core. Use several light strokes rather than bearing down on the knife. Then apply firm, even pressure to snap along the cut. Fold the cut portion back and slit the paper on the other side.

To cut an opening, first measure carefully. Then double check it. Remember which surface is the front and always measure from the top down. A technique that is sometimes helpful is to cover the edges of electrical boxes with chalk. Then transfer the chalk to the wallboard by pressing the panel against the wall. However, be sure to keep cuts on the front of the panel smooth, with no ripped paper.

Once the opening is marked, cut the sides with the utility knife and punch out with a hammer. Or, using a pointed wallboard saw, start the cut by plunging it through the panels well within the outline. For right angles mark the opening with a pencil and cut the shorter leg with a wallboard saw. Then cut and snap the re-

maining leg with the utility knife. For U-shaped openings first cut the two opposite legs with a saw and then cut and snap the remaining side with the knife.

Cut edges will often be slightly uneven. Don't waste time planing or chipping them smooth. Cut the panels 1/4 inch short in the first place. The jagged edges will fit together more easily, and the gap can be filled later with joint compound. Without enough clearance, attempts to force the panel in place will usually break the core and spoil the edge.

## Applying Panels

Apply the ceiling panels first. For this you need at least one helper, maybe two. (A 4-by-8 panel 1/2 inch thick weighs about 60 pounds.) Even with a helper, renting a wallboard jack or using two T-braces, called deadmen, is a good idea. Make the braces from 1 by 4s or 2 by 4s. The top of the T should be 2 to 3 feet wide, and the total length should be the floor-to-ceiling height plus 3/4 inch. Be careful not to gouge the paper surface of the panel. Another technique is to temporarily nail a 1 by 4 to the ceiling joist and use this as a lip for the edge of the wallboard. This carries some of the weight while the panel is nailed in place.

Position the length of the panel perpendicular to the ceiling joists. The edges should cover just half the width of the surrounding joists. Drive nails through the center of the panel first and then work around the perimeter. If you have difficulty sighting the joists, mark the panels with a pencil or snap a chalk line as a guide. The correct nailing pattern depends on the local building code. Check this beforehand. In many instances this is every 7 inches on ceiling panels and every 8 inches for walls. Along the perimeter the nails should be 3/8 to 1/2 inch from the edge. Once the nail is flush, give it one last blow to slightly dimple the surface but not hard enough to break the paper. This allows the nail heads to be covered with tape and joint compound. Don't countersink the nails or break the paper.

To cover the walls begin with an upper corner and position the panel flush with the ceiling. For vertical panels lift from the bottom edge with a foot lever, which is simply two pieces of 1 by 4 or shim stock used to create a fulcrum. If you're applying the panels horizontally, have a helper support some of the weight. Several nails or a wood block nailed beneath the lower edge of the panel can also serve as temporary supports.

Be sure the leading edge of the panel is vertical and covers just half the width of the last stud. If the corner isn't square, you can leave a gap of up to 1/2 inch, which can be covered with tape and joint compound.

If the studs are new wood, use two nails 2 inches apart spaced every 12 inches, instead of a single nail every 7 or 8 inches. This will minimize the chance of popped nails in the future.

Once the wall panels are in place, cover any outside corners with metal corner beads. Drive nails through the bead into the framing about every 5 or 6 inches. The nail heads and bead will be covered with joint compound.

## Using a T-Brace

T-braces help hold a ceiling panel in place for easier nailing.

## Using a Foot Fulcrum

A foot fulcrum can be made from a piece of tapered 1 by 4 and a short piece of 1 by 1. The fulcrum holds a wall panel against the ceiling for nailing. Commercially made fulcrums are available at stores that cater to the professional.

## Taping and Filling Joints

1. Fill the tapered-joint recess with joint compound. Use a 6'' knife.

2. Lay tape in the wet compound and press it flat. Add a little compound over the tape and let it dry for 24 hours.

3. Cover the tape with a second coat of compound. Let it dry thoroughly; then sand lightly.

4. Apply a final thin coat with a 10'' knife.

5. Sand lightly when dry.

6. Fill the nail dimples with compound. Two coats will be necessary.

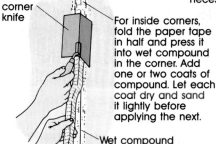

Inside corner knife

For inside corners, fold the paper tape in half and press it into wet compound in the corner. Add one or two coats of compound. Let each coat dry and sand it lightly before applying the next.

Wet compound

## Taping and Finishing

To cover the joints and nail heads, use the ready-mix joint compound that comes in gallon or 5-gallon containers. Use a separate container or mortarboard while applying the compound. Otherwise dried pieces will work their way into the fresh compound and make the job more difficult. In total you will put down three separate layers (each about 1/16-inch thick), gradually building the surface each time. Keep in mind that smooth, neat work at each stage is rewarded with less work in the long run and a better-looking finish job.

Using a 6-inch knife, cover all the nail holes in the center of the panels with joint compound. Next fill the gap between panels and spread a thin layer about 4 or 5 inches wide over the joint. Use your fingers or your knife to press a section of paper tape into the wet compound. Although the most efficient technique is to unroll the tape with one hand and use the other to smooth the tape with the knife, this takes practice. Feather out the edges and add a small amount of compound over the top of the paper. Be sure to eliminate any wrinkles or air bubbles. For inside corners apply compound to both sides. Then fold the paper in half, press into the corner, and smooth with the knife.

Let this first coat dry overnight. Repeat with a second coat 24 hours later, feathering out several inches on either side of the first coat. The total width of the joints is now 7 to 10 inches.

Use a 10-inch knife for the third and final coat. The width of the joints should be about 10 to 13 inches. For inside corners it's often easier to do one side at a time and let the compound dry. Then come back and do the other side.

After the compound is thoroughly dry, smooth the joints and nail heads with 80- or 100-grade sandpaper wrapped around a wood block. If you've done a careful job with the knives, there's little sanding to be done. Because the paper on the panels fuzzes easily, be sure to sand only the compound. An alternate technique that eliminates the gypsum dust is to use a wet sponge. This smooths the compound nicely as long as the surface isn't allowed to get too wet.

The next step is either painting or texturing. Texturing involves trowel techniques best left to a professional. Painting involves priming with a special latex sealer called PVA and finishing with a final coat or two of the chosen color.

# CONVERTING AN ATTIC

If you need additional living space, converting the attic may be a practical solution. The project can be cost-effective as well. A new addition built from the ground up requires its own foundation, framing, and roof. With an attic conversion these expensive essentials are already in place.

To begin the project, give some thought to how the space will be used. As a playroom for the children? An extra bedroom for guests? An office or studio? Don't be limited by preconceived ideas. An attic doesn't have to look like the rest of the house. In fact the unique architectural lines created by dormers and pitched ceilings are often part of an attic's special appeal. Also don't overlook unusual finishing possibilities. The space behind 4- or 5-foot walls, called *kneewalls,* can be used for built-in storage. Plan to take advantage of these areas under the eaves to maximize the available living space.

If you haven't already done so, research the local code regarding attic conversions. (For a discussion of codes, see page 24.) Ask the building department about any special restrictions or exceptions. For example, the requirements may be different for an attic used as a guest room rather than as a studio or office. Specifically there are five areas you should investigate.

■ *Minimum ceiling height.* Most codes say that at least 50 percent of the floor area in an attic used as habitable living space must have a minimum ceiling height of 7½ feet. (Utility and storage areas, workshops, bathrooms, and hallways aren't considered habitable living space—everything else is.) The minimum allowable height in the room, such as 4 or 5 feet, may be specified as well.

■ *Minimum room size.* Except for the kitchen, habitable living areas generally must be at least 7 feet wide, and 70 square feet in area.

■ *Allowable sizes and spans for floor joists.* The building code includes span charts to determine whether the floor system is structurally sound.

■ *Minimum width and allowable angle of the stairway.* Code requirements are different for main and service stairs. If the attic space is less than 400 square feet and used by fewer than 10 people, the existing stairs may be adequate. (If you need to build a new stairway, see page 62.)

■ *Number and size of windows and skylights.* If the attic is designated for sleeping, the code requires at least one operable window that can be used as an emergency fire exit. The window must be a minimum size and within a certain distance from the floor. The location and size of skylights is often determined by the code as well. (If you need to add a window or skylight, see pages 71 and 77.)

Once the minimum code requirements have been

**Floor Plan of the Proposed Attic Room**

**Finished Attic Room**

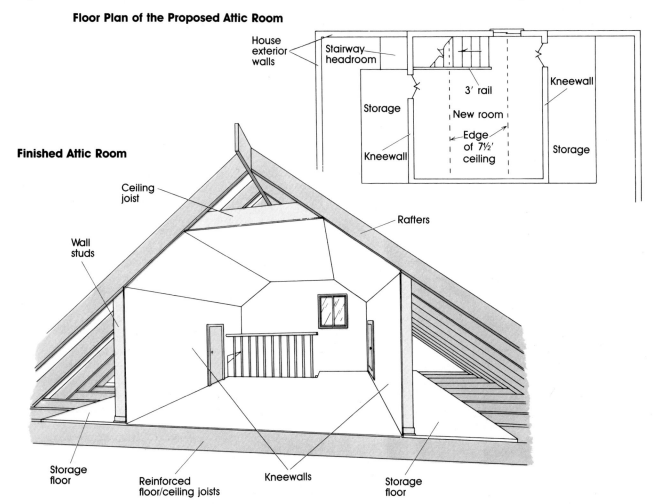

House exterior walls

Stairway headroom

3' rail

Kneewall

Storage

New room

Kneewall

Edge of 7½' ceiling

Storage

Ceiling joist

Rafters

Wall studs

Storage floor

Reinforced floor/ceiling joists

Kneewalls

Storage floor

determined, you can estimate the amount of usable space. This depends on the size of the house and the slope of the roof. *Slope* is measured as the number of inches of rise for every 12 inches of horizontal distance. If the slope is 6–12 (6 inches of rise for every 12 inches of horizontal distance) or less, the space is probably too small to be used for anything but storage.

Several key measurements should be made, and each depends on the code restrictions. As an example, let's assume the code requires at least 50 percent of the floor space to be over 7½ feet. The minimum allowable height is 4 feet. Begin by locating points along several rafters 8 feet above the existing joists. (The extra 6 inches is usually lost in the process of adding new joists and finishing the floor and ceiling.) Don't be concerned with collar beams that hang below the ceiling height. These can be relocated or removed later, as long as new structural members replace their function of keeping the rafters in place.

Measure the width and length of the resulting space and plot this on ¼-inch graph paper. Repeat the process at a 4½-foot height. If the space doesn't meet the 50 percent requirement, move in the kneewalls a foot or so. Although this cuts back on the total number of square feet, it also changes the ratio.

If the attic is large, you may be able to dispense with the kneewalls altogether and still have one or two good-sized rooms. With two rooms or more, allow space for a hallway so each room has its own separate entrance. Make the hall at least 3 feet wide so furniture can be moved easily.

If there are no stairs, allow space for adding them. Conventional straight-run stairs generally require an opening about 3 feet wide and 10 to 12 feet long. Prefabricated circular stairs need an opening from 4 to 6 feet square.

To help visualize the new space more easily, tack small nails to the sides of the corner rafters. Then use string to outline the perimeter of the room. Do this at the ceiling and kneewall heights. Stand in the space a while to see if it suits you. Is the additional living space you'll gain worth the cost of conversion?

## Building a New Floor

Many homes are built without anticipating future expansion in the attic. As a result the size of the existing joists is inadequate for living space. Joists that were intended as ceiling joists are large enough to carry the weight of the ceiling material underneath but nothing more. Now you need floor joists, strong enough to carry the additional load of walls, furnishings, and people walking back and forth.

Determining the correct joist size is an engineering problem. It's usually solved by simply checking the span charts in the code or by asking the building department for the proper size. In some situations you may need to consult with an architect or contractor. As a general rule if the existing joists are 2 by 4s or 2 by 6s, 16 inches on center, plan to build a new floor. If the joists are 2 by 8s, beef them up to carry the new load.

**Adding New Floor Joists**

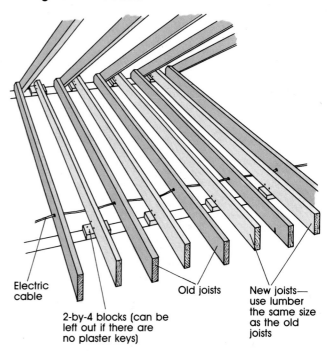

Electric cable

Old joists

New joists— use lumber the same size as the old joists

2-by-4 blocks (can be left out if there are no plaster keys)

Several techniques can be used to build the new floor system. The simplest is to nail the new joists to the side of the existing joists. One end of the new joist rests on the cap plate of the exterior walls. The other end rests on the same interior bearing wall where the old joists overlap. To prevent damage to the existing ceiling surface, raise the end of each joist with a ¾-inch block. This is especially important for lath-and-plaster ceilings with thick plaster keys. The joist ends must be cut to match the slope of the roofline. Use a bevel square or a cardboard template to determine the approximate angle. It doesn't have to be exact.

If the space between the old joists contains loose fill insulation, remove just enough to set the new joists in place. If insulating batts are used, pull them back or remove them altogether to allow nailing access.

Toenail the ends of each joist to the cap plate. If the angle of the roofline limits nailing access, drill starter holes at the end of the joist before nailing. Use a bit slightly smaller than the nail size. To connect the sides of the old and new joists, stagger 16d nails every 12 inches.

In some instances this technique may not work. If the ceiling surface below is lath and plaster, nailing into the old joists may jar and loosen the plaster. Or if there's a considerable amount of wiring running perpendicular to the existing joists, nailing new joists alongside probably isn't practical. If there aren't too many wires or the wiring is in bad shape anyway, pull it out and run new cable later. Generally, though, it's preferable to leave the existing electrical system intact whenever possible.

The alternative technique, which provides better sound isolation and reduces ceiling cracking, is to space the new joists evenly between the old. This creates a new floor system totally independent of the existing joists.

**Subfloor Plan of Proposed Attic Room**

**Nailing Subfloor Panels in Place**

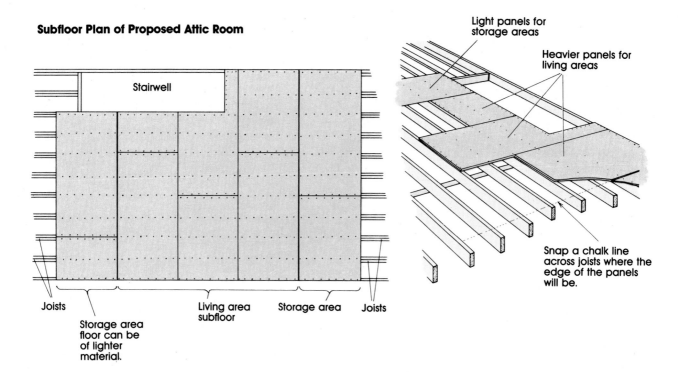

Raise the new joists with wood blocks as described previously. If necessary, use 2 by 4s laid flat to gain additional space to clear the existing wires. But keep in mind that each inch the floor is raised takes away valuable ceiling height. At the outer edges toenail the joists into the blocks and cap plate. Where the joists meet over the bearing wall, overlap the ends and nail together with 16d nails. Or butt the ends together and brace on both sides with 2-foot lengths of $3/8$-inch plywood. Double the joists under any future partition wall, but space them $3 1/2$ inches apart to allow for running new electrical cable.
**Utility systems.** Once the new floor joists are secured, any necessary utility systems should be roughed in. This process is done in two stages: before the subfloor goes down and after the walls are framed. Depending on the number of electrical outlets, you may need to run a completely new circuit from the service panel. If an existing circuit is well below capacity, it can be extended by running new cable into the attic space. Or perhaps you can tap a nearby junction box.

For heating it's best to consult a heating contractor. If the furnace capacity allows, perhaps you can extend an existing hot-air or hot-water system into the attic. Or you can install a separate electric baseboard heater. The contractor can advise you on the necessary equipment or actually install it.
**Subflooring.** After the utility systems are roughed in, the new subfloor can be installed. It's not necessary to cover the entire attic with subflooring—only the area to be finished. If you plan to use the eaves for storage, a permanent subfloor there is optional. Sheets of $1/2$-inch inexpensive grade plywood loose-laid over the eaves are often sufficient.

The choice of subfloor material depends on whether or not the finish floor requires a smooth surface. If it does, for resilient tile or sheet goods, use either $5/8$-inch CDX tongue-and-groove (T&G) plywood with a $5/16$-inch particle-board underlayment, or $3/4$-inch T&G plywood that has been plugged and touch sanded (PTS). If the finish floor, such as carpet or hardwood, can be laid over rough subflooring, the $5/8$-inch CDX T&G plywood is sufficient. In some cases, however, the $3/4$-inch T&G PTS plywood is actually cheaper. In all cases be sure the plywood is thick enough for the joist spacing. For instance, $5/8$-inch T&G is adequate for 16-inch joist spacings.

To begin sketch the subfloor layout on paper to minimize waste; design the subfloor to use full sheets of plywood wherever possible. Lay them with the smooth side up and the grain of the top sheet perpendicular to the joists. Stagger the end joints. To begin the installation start at one edge of the finish space and snap a chalk line along the joists as a guide. Apply a bead of construction adhesive to the tops of the joists. (This is optional but helps eliminate squeaks in the floor system.) Put down just enough adhesive for one panel at a time. Nail the subfloor to the joists with 8d nails spaced every 6 inches along the edges, 10 to 12 inches inside. Angle the nails slightly for a better grip. If you need a nailing guide, draw lines along the plywood or snap a chalk line. To position adjoining panels, leave $1/16$ inch of space between the ends and $1/8$ inch at the sides. This allows for expansion and for buckling.

## Framing Attic Walls

After the subfloor is installed, frame the walls. Begin by constructing the kneewalls under the eaves. The proper height for these is determined by three factors: the building code, preference, and practicality. If the code doesn't specify, you can choose almost any height, but a wall less than 4 feet high offers limited use of the space. Also keep in mind that if you choose a 4-foot kneewall, full panels can be installed horizontally. If you choose a 5-foot wall, buy 4-by-10 panels, cut them in half, and install the sections vertically.

Building a kneewall is similar to building a new partition wall (see page 49), except that the kneewall doesn't need a top plate. Begin by cutting a 2-by-4 sole plate the length of the new wall. Place the sole plate in position on the subfloor. Drop a plumb bob from each rafter to mark the plate for each stud. Also measure the distance from each rafter to the plate. If the distances vary less than ¼ inch, the studs can be face nailed to the side of the rafters. Cut all the studs the same length, square at both ends. If the distances vary more than ¼ inch, the tops of the studs should be cut at an angle and toenailed beneath each rafter. This technique is more time-consuming but takes the sag out of the roofline. As a result the finish wall and ceiling surface can be nailed to a smooth plane.

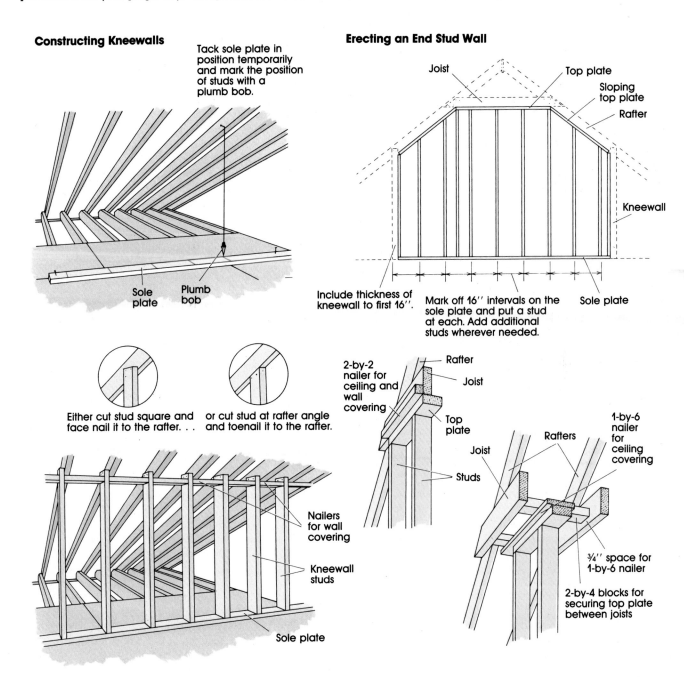

**Constructing Kneewalls**

Tack sole plate in position temporarily and mark the position of studs with a plumb bob.

Sole plate

Plumb bob

Either cut stud square and face nail it to the rafter. . .  or cut stud at rafter angle and toenail it to the rafter.

Nailers for wall covering

Kneewall studs

Sole plate

**Erecting an End Stud Wall**

Joist

Top plate

Sloping top plate

Rafter

Kneewall

Include thickness of kneewall to first 16''.

Mark off 16'' intervals on the sole plate and put a stud at each. Add additional studs wherever needed.

Sole plate

2-by-2 nailer for ceiling and wall covering

Rafter

Joist

Top plate

Studs

Joist

Rafters

1-by-6 nailer for ceiling covering

¾'' space for 1-by-6 nailer

2-by-4 blocks for securing top plate between joists

# A NEW STAIRWAY

Once you have the studs, place the sole plate on edge and drive two 16d nails into the ends of each stud. Lift and position the new wall and drive 16d nails through the sole plate and subfloor into the floor joists. Use a plumb bob or level to check the position and then drive 10d nails through the top of each stud into the rafter. Because there is no top plate above the studs, you must provide a nailing surface for wallboard or paneling. Cut and toenail short lengths of 2 by 4s between the rafters.

Two ceiling treatments are possible at this point. One is a pitched ceiling all the way to the peak, and the other a horizontal drop ceiling at least 7½ feet high. For a pitched, or vaulted, ceiling the existing rafters and collar beams serve as main framing members. The exposed collar beams must be at least 6 feet 8 inches from the floor and spaced no more than 4 feet apart. If they are too low, or if you want more attractive beams, raise or replace them one at a time. In any case do not remove collar beams altogether without being certain the knee-walls provide sufficient structural support.

For a horizontal drop ceiling, install ceiling joists high enough so there will be at least 7½ feet of head-room after finish ceiling and floor materials are installed. These joists can be 2 by 4s or 2 by 6s. Check the span charts in the building code. If the existing collar beams are below the ceiling height, replace them one at a time with new joists. Locate the correct ceiling height on the rafter by dropping a plumb bob and measuring along it. Repeat the process to mark the opposing rafter and measure the distance between them.

The ends of the joists should be cut at an angle to maximize the nailing surface. Use a bevel square to find the approximate angle—it doesn't have to be exact. Allow ¼-inch clearance at either end and cut the joists with a hand or circular saw. If the joists are slightly bowed, the crown or high side should be to the top. With a helper, lift the joist into place and then drive a 16d nail through the joist into the rafter. After checking the position to be certain it's level, secure the joist by nailing both ends with at least three nails.

To erect regular partition walls, follow the procedures described on page 49. The sole plate in this case will be longer than the top plate. The sole plate runs between the two kneewalls; the top plate fits between the sloping rafters. The framing is simplified if the wall is positioned directly beneath one of the new ceiling joists. Be sure to provide a nailing surface for wallboard. If the wall must be positioned between joists, install 2-by-4 nailing blocks first. To provide a nailing surface, raise the blocks ¾ inch and nail a 1 by 6 between the blocks and the top plate.

Nail 2 by 2s along the side of the sloping rafter between the kneewalls and partition wall. Then nail a 2 by 4 to the bottom of the rafter, creating a sloping top plate. Next measure and cut the studs necessary to fill the gap between the two walls. Toenail these studs to the top and sole plates with two 8d nails on each side. Check all corner assemblies for sufficient nailing surfaces. Add 2-by-4 nailers as needed.

Installing a new stairway is not a casual weekend project. The job demands thorough planning, numerous mathematical calculations, and careful carpentry. The degree of craftsmanship required to build an elaborate, decorative stairway can enter the realm of fine cabinet-work, which is beyond the scope of this book. This section does describe, however, the basic procedure for building a conventional, straight-run stairway suitable for attic or basement access.

Before you decide to build the stairs yourself, investigate some options and compare prices. It's possible to provide a stair manufacturer with specific dimensions and have a complete set of stairs prefabricated and delivered. The manufacturer can install the stairs, or you can do this yourself. A second option is to hire a contractor to install prebuilt stairs or to custom build stairs on the site. A third possibility is to take your dimensions to a building supplier or stair manufacturer and order many of the parts precut. This is especially true for finishing details such as hardwood balusters, posts, and railings.

As with many other projects, you should begin by checking the local building code. If the stairway is considered to be main stairs, most codes require a minimum 32-inch width between the handrails. Minimum head-room is 6 feet 8 inches. For stairs serving fewer than 10 people, the minimum width is usually 30 inches and the headroom 6 feet 4 inches. But keep in mind that these are minimum requirements only. If you have the space to spare, increase the dimensions for convenient and comfortable use. Two people can pass safely on stairs 36 inches wide; headroom of 7 feet to 7 feet 4 inches generally allows plenty of access for moving furniture up and down.

A handrail is required on at least one side of the stairway—on both sides for stairways wider than 4 feet. It should be a consistent 30 to 34 inches above the nosing of each step. (The *nosing* is the edge of the tread that extends beyond the riser. The amount of overhang varies, depending on the thickness of the tread.) The handrail should be terminated at both ends in such a way that cuffs and loose clothing will not catch on it. There should be a 1½-inch clearance between handrail and wall.

If a doorway is planned at the top of the stairs, swing it away from the stairs or include a 3-foot landing. Plan a minimum of 3 feet between the top or bottom steps and an adjacent wall. This provides room for entering and leaving the stairs and for moving furniture.

## Where to Locate the Stairway

One logical place to locate a stairway is directly above an existing stairway. For example, a new set of stairs to the attic can often be located above the main stairs or basement stairs. If this isn't practical, position the stairs so the length is parallel to the direction of the joists. This greatly simplifies the framing process. If the stairs must run perpendicular to the joists, it's preferable to position them along a bearing wall, or to add posts or a new wall to support the trimmer joists.

If you don't have the space for conventional stairs, consider prefabricated circular stairs. The units come in

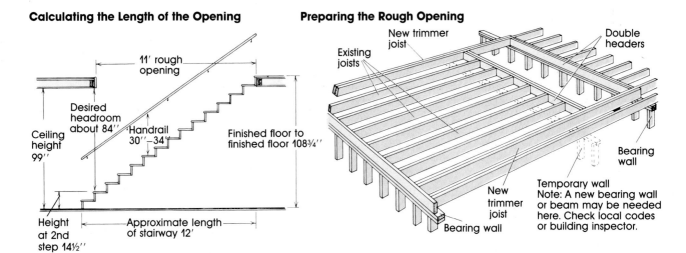

**Calculating the Length of the Opening**

11' rough opening

Desired headroom about 84''

Ceiling height 99''

Handrail 30''–34''

Finished floor to finished floor 108¾''

Height at 2nd step 14½''

Approximate length of stairway 12'

**Preparing the Rough Opening**

New trimmer joist

Existing joists

Double headers

Bearing wall

New trimmer joist

Bearing wall

Temporary wall Note: A new bearing wall or beam may be needed here. Check local codes or building inspector.

a kit, with complete assembly and framing instructions provided by the manufacturer. Diameters range from 4 to 6 feet. Check the code first to find the minimum size allowed. One obvious liability with circular stairs is difficulty moving large pieces of furniture. But in some situations you may have no choice.

### Determining Rise and Run

The local code specifies the acceptable depth and height of the steps. To define some basic terms, the *tread* is the horizontal step; its depth is called the *unit run*. The *riser* is the vertical member between the steps; its height is called the *unit rise*. The correct relationship between these two is absolutely essential for proper stair construction. If the ratio is incorrect, the stairs will be either too steep or too shallow, and consequently uncomfortable and unsafe.

For main stairs most codes specify risers between 7 and 7½ inches; the tread should be 10 to 11 inches. For secondary stairs the maximum allowable rise is usually 8 inches; the minimum tread is 9 inches. Added together, the tread and riser should total 17 to 18 inches.

To determine the proper rise and run, measure accurately from finish floor to finish floor. This distance includes the floor-to-ceiling height, plus the depth of the joists, subfloor, and finish floor. If no opening exists, drill a small hole through the ceiling and floor material. If the finish floor is not installed, find the proper depth and adjust your measurement. (For attic stairs add the depth of the finish floor; for basements subtract it.) In the case of an attic conversion, be sure to use the depth of the new floor system, not the existing ceiling joists.

Next convert this measurement to inches and divide by 7. Let's say the floor-to-floor height is 108¾ inches. Dividing by 7 yields about 15½. Because you must have a whole number of risers, drop the fraction. Now divide 108¾ inches by 15 risers to get the exact riser height. The answer is 7¼ inches.

We know that the tread and riser must total 17 to 18 inches. So to determine the tread size, subtract 7¼ from 17½ to get 10¼. Because the last riser leads to the finish floor and not another tread, there is one more riser than tread. In this case you will have 14 treads. To find the total run, or length of the stairs, simply multiply the number of treads by the unit run (14 times 10¼ inches). The total length is 143½ inches, or approximately 12 feet.

### Preparing the Rough Opening

Carefully study the sketches illustrating the proper framing for the rough opening. If possible, position the opening along existing joists. If the joist spacing and the desired width won't allow this, add one or two sets of double joists to achieve the proper size.

In calculating the width of the rough opening, take into account the width of any handrails required by the code. Also include the thickness of any finish material to be applied later, such as wallboard or paneling.

The length of the opening depends on the minimum headroom. To continue the previous example, let's assume the ceiling height is 99 inches. If the desired headroom is 7 feet (84 inches), you have 15 inches to work with. With a riser height of 7¼ inches, the minimum headroom is reached over the second step (7¼ times 2 equals 14½ inches). The rough opening will extend from the top of the stairs to the edge of the second step. If a shorter opening is desired, lower the minimum headroom and recalculate.

Begin framing the rough opening by installing the trimmer joists. In a basement location these should be the same size and length as the existing joists. If necessary, plane the lower edge of the trimmer slightly to get it in position. Then shim the ends so the top of the trimmer is tight against the subfloor. Nail to the existing joist by driving 16d nails every 12 inches or so. To add two new trimmers, it's generally easier to lift and install one at a time. Blocking should be nailed between the ends of the joists and in the middle of the span.

For an attic location the trimmers should be the same size as the new floor joists (see page 58). The process of installing the new floor system and framing the stair opening can be done at the same time.

Mark the edges of the rough opening by drilling corner holes up through the subfloor or down through the ceiling. Add the width of the double headers to be installed at both ends of the opening. Four headers, each 1½ inches wide, will add 6 inches to the cut.

Remove the ceiling or floor material within the opening. Once the joists are exposed, but before they are cut, build two temporary supports to carry the load (see page 42). If the stairs run parallel to the joists, short lengths of 3 feet or less generally don't need bracing. If the stairs run perpendicular to the joists, it may be necessary to cut through six or seven joists. So provide temporary braces on both sides with the studs shimmed tightly between the plates. Position the supports about 12 inches from the edge of the opening. If a new wall is to be built flanking the stairway, erect the wall now instead of temporary supports. (Follow the procedure described on page 49 for building a new partition wall.)

With a square, mark the joists to be removed and cut with a handsaw or reciprocating saw. If possible, use these cut portions for the double headers. If not, cut new headers to fit snugly between the trimmer joists. Nail two headers together and secure them to the trimmers and the cut tail joists with joist hangers. With this done the rough opening is complete.

## Cutting Stringers

Stringers for the stairs described here are generally cut from 2 by 12s. To allow for trimming, order them 24 inches longer than the finish length. The simplest stairway has two stringers with 1-by-3 cleats nailed or screwed to the sides. Then treads, but no risers, are nailed to the cleats. Or the stringers can be dadoed to accept the thickness of the tread. The dado cuts should not be deeper than one-third the thickness of the stringers. An alternative technique that creates a strong closed stairway calls for cutting the stringers into a sawtooth pattern. The risers and treads are supported by the cutouts and nailed to the stringers.

Treads are usually precut 1⅛-inch hardwood or Douglas fir. The nosing extends over the riser an inch or so. Risers are generally ¾-inch matching stock. If the stairs are to be carpeted, however, the treads can be 2 by 12s cut to fit, and the risers ¾-inch plywood.

Use a framing square to mark the cuts for the first stringer. Measure off the tread dimension along one edge and the riser dimension on the other. With these two marks directly over the edge of the stringer, mark the outline with a sharp pencil. Continue the process until all risers and treads are laid out. This demands care because the finish steps must meet a ¼-inch tolerance to pass the building inspection.

Double check all markings and then cut the first stringer with a saw. When using a power saw, finish each cut with a handsaw to get it square.

To ensure that the first step will be the same height as the others, trim the bottom of the stringer by the thickness of one tread (see illustration). Also mark the bottom edge for a 1½- by 3½-inch notch. This is for a 2-by-4 kicker that anchors the stringers to the floor. If the stringers are to be supported at the top by a 2-by-4 ledger, cut a second notch.

Place the stringer in the rough opening to see if it fits properly. Once it does, use it as a pattern for the other stringer. For stairs over 36 inches wide, a third stringer is

### Building a Stairway

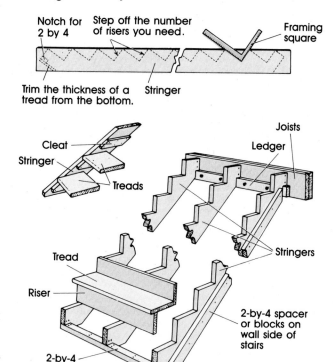

Notch for 2 by 4

Step off the number of risers you need.

Framing square

Trim the thickness of a tread from the bottom.

Stringer

Cleat

Stringer

Treads

Joists

Ledger

Stringers

Tread

Riser

2-by-4 spacer or blocks on wall side of stairs

2-by-4 cleat

required to provide additional support in the center. It is advisable even for narrower stairs. A simple option is to run a 2 by 4 under the middle of the stairs in lieu of a cutout stringer. If on one or both sides stringers are being attached to wall studs, fasten a 2-by-4 spacer to the studs. That way there is room to slip wallboard and a 1-by-12 finish stringer between the cutout stringer and the studs.

Now install the stringers. At the top, nail a 2-by-4 ledger to the header with 16d nails and fit the notched stringers over it. Or butt the stringers directly up against the header and secure with metal joist hangers. Secure the stringers to the sidewalls by driving 16d nails into the 2-by-4 space. Nail the kicker to the floor and toenail the stringers. If the floor is concrete, drill holes for expansion shields and attach the kicker with lag bolts. Any wood in contact with concrete should be pressure-treated or coated with preservative first.

Once the stringers are secured, install the treads and risers, allowing clearance for applying wallboard and finish stringer later. Starting from the bottom, nail two or three risers to the stringers with 8d finishing nails. Apply construction adhesive to each joint before nailing. Then nail corresponding treads to the stringers. From the back, nail each riser to the tread with 8d nails spaced about every 8 inches. If the tread and riser are hardwood, predrill the holes with a bit slightly smaller than the nail size. Otherwise the wood will split.

After you have finished the wall surface, you can install a railing. Use milled stock and standard brackets that can be attached to the studs with wood screws. The top of the railing should be a consistent 30 to 34 inches above the nosing of each step.

# FINISHING A BASEMENT

An existing basement is a prime candidate for expanding the living area in your home. (This means a full-size basement under at least a portion of your house. If there is only crawl space it's generally more practical to build an addition aboveground than to excavate under the house.) One obvious advantage is that the basement is already enclosed with a rough floor, outside walls, and ceiling joists. Access usually isn't a problem because most basements already have a stairway. The basement is often as large as the living area on the first floor, so the potential for converting the space is great.

Many basement remodelings, however, run into complications. These typically include excess moisture, masonry walls and floors, and an assortment of exposed pipes and ducts. This section describes a number of techniques you can use to overcome these problems and prepare the basement for finishing.

Code limitations for a basement conversion are similar to those for attics. Before you begin, check your local code regarding ceiling heights and stairways. The intended use of an area is often the key factor. If you don't plan to use the basement as habitable livng space, the ceiling restrictions are usually less demanding.

## Eliminating Excess Moisture

The most critical problem in any basement remodeling is excess moisture. This has to be resolved satisfactorily before you can proceed with your plans. If your basement has a moisture problem, start with an outside inspection. Check all downspouts and gutters to be sure they're in good working condition. If you don't have splash blocks or extensions to carry the water away from the house, buy some. Check the perimeter of the house to be sure the grading slopes away from the foundation. Look for low spots where water can accumulate, especially around window wells. Check the seal around the bottom of doors and basement windows and recaulk as necessary.

From the inside, examine the basement walls and floor for cracks. To repair cracks, dig out a 1/2- to 1-inch groove with a cold chisel. If possible, make the inside of the groove slightly wider than the outside. This prevents the patching material from falling out too easily. With a stiff wire brush, clean away loose material from the opening. Wet down the sides so the surrounding material won't leach water from the new mortar. Then apply a small batch of hydraulic cement, mixed according to

**An Unfinished Basement**

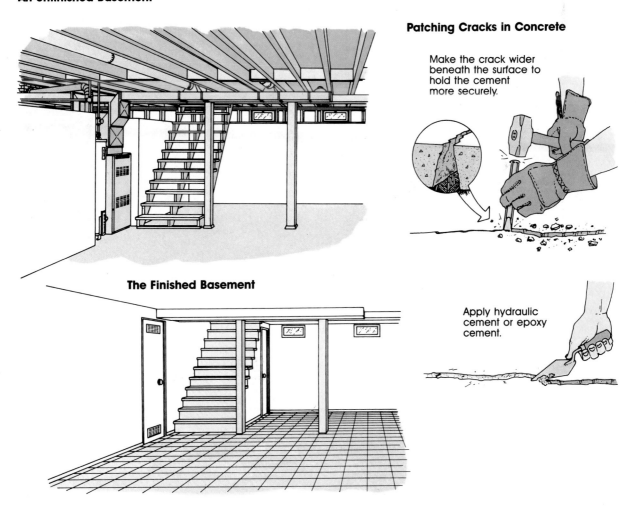

**Patching Cracks in Concrete**

Make the crack wider beneath the surface to hold the cement more securely.

**The Finished Basement**

Apply hydraulic cement or epoxy cement.

the manufacturer's instructions. This is readily available from most hardware stores and building suppliers.

The joints between the walls and floor are a common problem, so inspect these areas carefully. If the joint is the source of leaks, widen it slightly and fill with an epoxy cement. Once the epoxy has dried, cover with patching cement.

If the mortar between concrete blocks is loose and crumbling, the joints should be repointed. Use a ready-mix mortar or mix your own with 1 part masonry cement and 3 parts fine sand. With a cold chisel dig out about 1/2 to 3/4 inch of the old mortar. Then wet the joint and pack in as much new mortar as you can. A special tuck-pointing tool works best. The mortar will cure better if kept moist, so cover it with damp burlap, or spray it lightly several times a day for 4 or 5 days.

After all these repairs, coat the wall and floor with a waterproof sealer. This could be an alkyd-based cement paint or a sealer made of silicone or epoxy. Most sealers go on like paint and can be applied with a brush or roller. If you cover a large surface with epoxy, be sure to provide adequate ventilation.

If you find no cracks but the basement is obviously damp, the problem is either seepage or condensation. Cut a 12-inch square of heavy plastic or aluminum foil and tape it to the basement wall below ground level (below grade). Leave it in place for several days and then remove it. If you find that the area under the square is wet, the problem is seepage. If the area underneath is dry, but the surrounding wall is damp, the problem is condensation.

Solving a seepage problem is not always possible from the inside. You can try coating the walls and floor with a waterproof sealer, but the results can't be guaranteed. If the moisture problem persists, the job may require a more radical solution. Your best bet is to call a contractor who is familiar with the moisture problems in your area. You may need to excavate and waterproof the exterior of the foundation. If the soil is clay or another material that drains poorly, a system of drainage tiles may be needed to carry excess water from the house. If the water table is too high, nothing much can be done except to install a sump pump and forget about finishing the basement.

If the problem is condensation, there is too much humidity in the air. First remove any obvious sources of moisture. For example, a clothes dryer in the basement should be vented to the outdoors. To prevent pipes from sweating, insulate the cold-water pipes with wrapping tape or neoprene sleeves. Leave the basement windows open when the weather allows, or improve the ventilation by installing a ventilating fan in a window opening. If these efforts aren't enough, install an electric dehumidifier to remove excess moisture from the air.

■ *A note of caution:* with any remedy for a moisture problem, wait several months or through a rainy season before you assume a permanent cure. The problem should be completely solved before you begin your remodeling.

## Preparing the Floor Surface

If the concrete floor in the basement is dry and reasonably smooth, you may be able to apply the finish floor directly over the concrete. Ceramic tile, indoor/outdoor carpet, and some types of resilient tiles, for example, are suitable for use below grade over concrete. Minor pits and low spots should be filled first with patching cement. With the application of a waterproof sealer, the floor is ready for finishing.

In many cases, however, a new subfloor should be built over the concrete. A new subfloor is required if:
■ The existing floor is damp due to condensation and high humidity.
■ The concrete is rough, uneven, sloped, or badly cracked.
■ Other types of finish flooring are desired, such as sheet vinyl, most types of carpeting, and wood flooring.
■ You prefer a subfloor above the concrete to make the finish floor warmer and more comfortable to walk on.

Two techniques can be used to install a subfloor over concrete. Both methods are similar—the choice is primarily a matter of preference and may depend on the materials you have at hand.

**Installing the subfloor.** Sweep the floor clean and then spread a layer of roofing asphalt over the entire surface. Make this about 1/4 inch thick (the depth need not be exact or the layer perfectly smooth). Lay heavy building paper or sheets of 6-mil polyethylene over the asphalt. Overlap the edges about 6 inches. Snap chalk lines 16 inches on center across the width of the floor. Then lay lengths of 2 by 4s along the chalk lines. These can be random lengths or scraps you've been saving. (Be sure the thicknesses are the same.) The wood should be treated with preservative beforehand. Leaving 1/4 to 1/2 inch between the ends of the 2 by 4s to allow for air circulation, secure them to the floor with concrete nails. They won't be tight, but the nail points will dig into the concrete enough to keep the sleepers from sliding

### Installing a Basement Subfloor

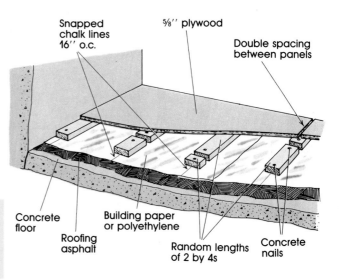

Snapped chalk lines 16″ o.c.

5/8″ plywood

Double spacing between panels

Concrete floor

Roofing asphalt

Building paper or polyethylene

Random lengths of 2 by 4s

Concrete nails

around once the plywood is applied. At this point you're ready to apply a ⅝-inch plywood subfloor, as described on page 59. *Be sure to double the recom-mended spacing between panels to allow for the extra humidity in the air.*

**An alternative technique.** Sweep the floor clean and then apply a waterproofing sealant with a brush or roller. When the sealant is dry, snap chalk lines 16 inches apart across the width of the floor. Along these marks, apply a mastic suitable for bonding wood to concrete. The easiest method is to buy mastic in a tube and use a caulking gun. Lay random lengths of 1 by 2s over the mastic (1 by 3s or 1 by 4s can also be used). Treat them with preservative first or use pressure-treated lumber. Leave a ¼- to ½-inch gap between ends and drive concrete nails into the floor every 24 inches. When the entire floor is covered, spread a layer of plastic (4- or 6-mil polyethylene) over the sleepers. Overlap the joints 6 inches. Then add a second layer of untreated 1 by 2s and nail them to the sleepers below. Once this is completed lay the plywood subfloor as described previously.

## Preparing the Walls

In most instances it's desirable to cover the basement walls with a finish material such as wallboard or paneling. The advantages are twofold: improved appearance and added insulation against the cold exterior walls. In mild climates the dead air space between the finish wall and the masonry is sufficient. In colder areas you should plan to add batts or rigid panels to improve the insulation (see page 53). If you do, the finished basement will be more comfortable and your heating bills will be lower.

Before the walls can be finished, however, you must add a nailing surface over the masonry. This can be accomplished with furring strips—normally 1 by 2s laid flat against a wall—or with a new false wall built in front of the existing foundation wall. The choice depends on a number of factors. In general, furring strips can be used in the following cases.

■ *If the walls are flat and plumb.* Check the foundation with a plumb bob or a long level and straight 2 by 4. If the walls are reasonably straight and plumb, fine. Minor problems can be corrected with shim stock behind the furring strips. Otherwise it's more practical to frame a new wall in front of the old.

■ *If you don't need to install more than ¾ inch of insulation.* Furring strips laid against the wall usually allow a ¾-inch space for installing rigid insulating panels or 1½-inch batts compressed to fit. Check the necessary R-value in your area. If you need additional thickness, use a false wall instead of furring.

■ *If there have been no serious moisture problems.* Attaching the strips to the wall with nails or screws could aggravate problems such as leaking cracks or seepage and cause new leaking.

## Installing Furring Strips

If you're using insulation batts or no insulation at all, first cover the wall with a plastic moisture barrier (see page 53). The barrier should be 4-mil polyethylene sheets with

## Installing Furring Strips

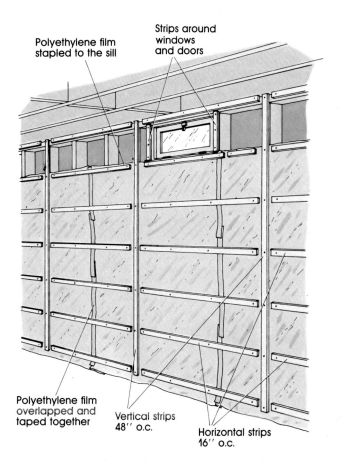

Polyethylene film stapled to the sill

Strips around windows and doors

Polyethylene film overlapped and taped together

Vertical strips 48″ o.c.

Horizontal strips 16″ o.c.

the joints overlapped and taped tight. Cut the sheets an extra inch or two long and trim the bottom later. Staple the top to the edge of the sill. Next snap vertical chalk lines 48 inches on center. Along each line attach 1-by-2 furring strips with 1½-inch concrete nails every 16 inches. Or you can use lead or fiber expansion shields and wood screws instead. Position these 36 inches apart. Snap horizontal chalk lines 16 inches apart. As you install these short pieces of furring, leave a ¼-inch gap between the ends to allow for air circulation. Be sure to fur completely around any window openings. If you are using insulating batts, install the paper or foil vapor barrier facing toward the inside of the room. If the batts are unfaced, add a vapor barrier of plastic sheets after the insulation is in place.

If you're using rigid insulating panels, install the furring first. The space between the furring can be modified to fit the dimensions of the panels, but keep in mind you also need a nailing surface for the finish wall. Glue the panels to the foundation wall according to the manufacturer's instructions. Then apply a plastic vapor barrier over the strips and panels. Because this furring is in contact with masonry, it should be redwood, pressure-treated, or coated with some wood preservative before installation.

## Building a False Wall

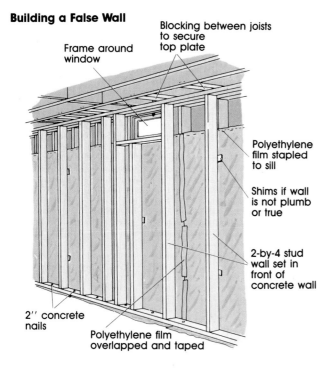

Frame around window

Blocking between joists to secure top plate

Polyethylene film stapled to sill

Shims if wall is not plumb or true

2-by-4 stud wall set in front of concrete wall

2'' concrete nails

Polyethylene film overlapped and taped

## Building a False Wall

If you choose to build a false wall in front of the existing foundation, review the instructions on page 49 for erecting a new wall. This process varies from new wall construction in only a few ways.

■ First cover the foundation wall with a plastic moisture barrier stapled to the sill. Cut the sheets long enough to lap under the sole plate.

■ If the foundation is out of plumb or not flat, use shim stock or 1-by-2 blocks behind the wall.

■ If a pipe runs along the exterior wall, use 1-by-2 or 2-by-4 blocks to clear the obstruction.

■ If the floor is concrete, attach the sole plate with 2-inch concrete nails 16 inches on center. If a new subfloor has been installed, 10d common nails are sufficient.

## Hiding Pipes and Ducts

If you're fortunate, the exposed overhead pipes and heating ducts run between the joists, tucked above the bottom edge. If you're not so lucky, the pipes and ducts hang below the joists, which creates a problem in finishing the ceiling. In some cases you may be able to reroute or raise the offending pipes beween the joists. As a rule this isn't practical if more than one or two pipes are involved. Often the ductwork is so large it can't be moved elsewhere anyway.

The easiest solution to the problem is a suspended ceiling. Installation is simple, and when you buy the components complete instructions are generally provided by the manufacturer. The process involves nailing

## Framing Around Ductwork

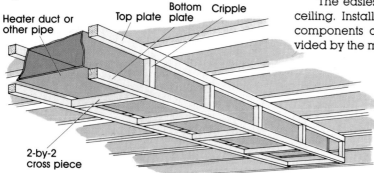

Heater duct or other pipe

Top plate

Bottom plate

Cripple

2-by-2 cross piece

## Installing a Suspended Ceiling

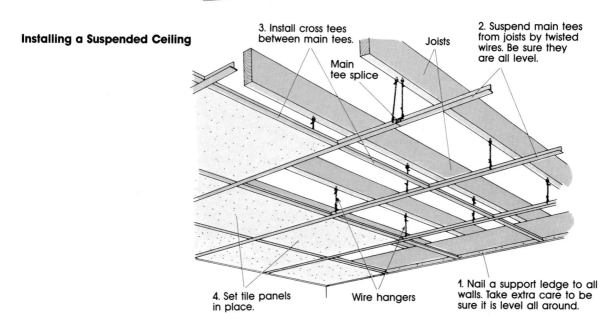

3. Install cross tees between main tees.

Main tee splice

Joists

2. Suspend main tees from joists by twisted wires. Be sure they are all level.

4. Set tile panels in place.

Wire hangers

1. Nail a support ledge to all walls. Take extra care to be sure it is level all around.

## Building an Access Panel

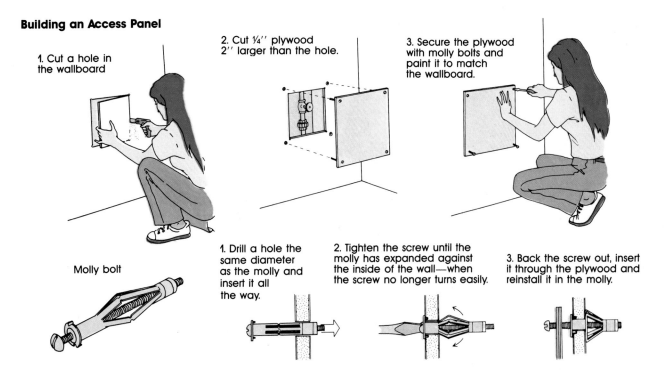

1. Cut a hole in the wallboard

2. Cut ¼'' plywood 2'' larger than the hole.

3. Secure the plywood with molly bolts and paint it to match the wallboard.

Molly bolt

1. Drill a hole the same diameter as the molly and insert it all the way.

2. Tighten the screw until the molly has expanded against the inside of the wall—when the screw no longer turns easily.

3. Back the screw out, insert it through the plywood and reinstall it in the molly.

a metal molding around the perimeter of the room and suspending two or three main runners from the joists with screw eyes and wire every 4 feet. Cross tees fit into slots on the runners to complete the grid. Ceiling tiles, usually 2 by 2 or 2 by 4 feet, are slipped into the framework and rest on the edges of the tees and runners. If necessary, a portion of the grid can be dropped even lower than the rest of the ceiling to accommodate a particular group of pipes or ducts.

In basement remodeling, three advantages recommend a suspended ceiling over a conventional wallboard ceiling. (1) Because the tiles can be removed and replaced in a matter of minutes, all the pipes and ducts remain accessible. This is essential if emergency repairs to the plumbing or heating system become necessary. (2) Because the grid is suspended from the joists rather than nailed to them, the bottom surface of the joists doesn't have to be smooth or level. (With an irregular surface a wallboard installation requires furring strips and shimming.) (3) The tiles add a level of soundproofing that can be beneficial in a workshop or recreation area.

A suspended ceiling does have one disadvantage: it takes up about 3 to 4 inches of ceiling height. If headroom is at a premium, you may need to box in certain pipes and ducts instead, but the box must be at least 6 feet 8 inches from the floor. The process is much like building a small partition wall. One technique is to cover a long duct hanging below the joists by building two identical frameworks from 2 by 2s, as illustrated. Each is complete with a top and bottom plate and short cripple studs 16 inches on center. Attach each frame to the ceiling by nailing the top plate to the bottom of the joists. Cut short lengths of 2 by 2s the width of the duct and nail them between the two frames.

An alternative technique is to assemble all three sides on the floor. Then with a helper lift and nail the unit in place. The frame can be covered with ceiling tiles, wallboard, or paneling. The size of the framework can vary—simply make it strong enough to support the finish material. You may be able to box some pipes or ducts with wooden lattices constructed from 1 by 2s or 1 by 3s.

Use the same type of framework to cover vertical pipes in a corner or along the wall. Nail the plates to the ceiling and floor as you would a full-size wall. With some imagination and slightly more effort, you can also build a storage closet or bookcase to fit around the pipes. These solutions do double duty: they camouflage the pipes and are functional as well. Room projections must be a minimum of 6 feet 8 inches from the finish floor.

When finishing the walls and ceilings, keep in mind that all shutoff and drain valves, cleanout plugs, meters, and electrical junction boxes must remain accessible. Building an access panel in a wallboard surface is simple. First cut out an opening with a wallboard or keyhole saw. Then cut a piece of ¼-inch plywood 2 inches larger than the opening. For example, if the access hole is 10 inches square, make the plywood 12 inches square. Hold the panel in place and drill for Molly bolts at each corner. Once the panel is secured to the wall, it can be removed and replaced at any time simply by unscrewing the Mollys. If the plywood is painted to match the rest of the wall, it will be barely noticeable.

Before any pipes are covered, it's a good idea to inspect the entire plumbing system. Make sure there are no leaks or corrosion that can stain the finish surfaces. Overlooking even minor drips means trouble later on, so take care of repairs before finishing begins. You should also insulate cold-water pipes to prevent condensation and hot-water pipes to save energy.

# MAKING EXTERIOR CHANGES

Beyond painting and roofing, you may
find good reasons to work on the outside
of your house: expanding floor space,
adding a window, or putting in new
doors. A simple skylight may completely
change how you use a room.

This chapter concerns changes that affect exterior parts of the house. The change may be a modest skylight barely noticeable from the street, or it may be a dramatic second-floor addition that alters your entire home.

In this chapter you will learn how to make cosmetic changes, such as a new window or sliding glass door. You will also learn how to expand the living space in your home, either by converting a garage or by building a room addition outward, upward, or downward.

## Adding a New Window

New windows come in a wide range of sizes and styles. The catalog of one manufacturer, for example, lists more than 200 different stock sizes. If you need a nonstandard size, windows can be custom milled, so the choices are practically unlimited. In fact, you may spend more time selecting a new window than actually installing it.

Four basic styles of windows are available: double-hung, casement, gliding, and awning. Each style can be used alone or combined in a number of variations.

■ *The double-hung window* is the most common and perhaps most traditional style. It consists of two movable sashes, one above the other, that slide up and down in wood or metal channels. Half of the window area can be opened at a time. The old-style double-hungs employ a sash cord and balance weight concealed in the wall cavity. The newer styles, since about 1950, operate on counterbalanced springs and a metal track.

■ *The casement window* has single or double sashes hinged on the side so that the entire window area swings out from the house to catch the breeze. Older casement windows push in and out; newer models are cranked open and shut.

■ *The gliding window* looks like a horizontal casement but operates like a double-hung unit. The sashes slide from side to side on plastic or metal tracks.

◀

Most prefabricated skylights are made with domes or panes of clear or tinted glass.

■ *The awning window* is hinged near the top and swings out from the bottom. This style offers the advantage that it can be left open during the rain.

Selecting a new window depends on several factors. A primary consideration is the type of windows already in place. If possible, the new unit should be an identical match or at least compatible in style, proportion, and material to the existing windows. Mixing a large aluminum casement with multipane double-hung wood windows can spoil the exterior appearance of the house.

Energy conservation is another important consideration. Double-glazed windows have two panes of glass permanently sealed in the sash to create an insulating air space. This cuts heat loss through the glass area by almost half and minimizes winter moisture problems such as fogging and condensation. If you live in a hot or cold climate, by all means consider double glazing. (In some areas the code demands it.) Triple glazing can be a worthwhile investment in certain areas.

Most window styles are available in either wood or metal. As a rule wood offers better insulation than metal. Although the heat flow through aluminum is 1,700 times faster than through wood, more expensive metal windows are now constructed with a thermal barrier between the inside and outside frame. Check heat loss carefully when you compare models and prices.

Maintenance is a third factor to consider. Baked or anodized finishes on aluminum windows require no upkeep. Wood exposed to the weather requires periodic care. One compromise is to choose a wood window encased in rigid vinyl. These top-of-the-line windows combine the superior insulating qualities of wood with the no-maintenance advantages of plastic.

## Removing a Window

The steps in removing a window are basically the same for all styles. Since double-hung windows are the most common, they're used here to illustrate the process.

First remove the interior stops that hold the lower

sash in place. Use a flat bar or broad wood chisel to pry the stops from the jambs. If the edges are lapped with paint, sever the joint with a sharp utility knife. Next remove the interior trim around the window. If the corners are mitered, try to drive the finish nails completely through with a small nail set. Often the interior trim can be reused once the new window is installed, so handle

these pieces with care. Use a flat bar to gently pry the side and top trim from the wall. Wrap a wood block in cloth to gain leverage and yet protect the wall surface from gouging. If the window has an interior stool— most double-hung windows do—raise the lower sash and pry or tap the stool from underneath to loosen and remove it.

From this point the correct procedure depends on the window. Examining the type of installation will tell you how to proceed. Older windows are often built in place with the jambs and exterior casings nailed to the studs. Newer windows are installed as a unit with nails through the exterior casing securing the window to the studs. Prying the casing loose should free the entire unit.

If the nails in the exterior casing are visible, drive them through the wood with a nail set. Or use a flat bar to pry the casings from the studs. Sever any surrounding caulk with a chisel. Pry the casings loose from the rest of the window and remove them. This should expose the nails securing the jambs to the studs. If there's room, slip a hacksaw blade into the opening and cut the nails. Use a chisel to pound out any shim stock hiding the nails.

### Removing an Old Window

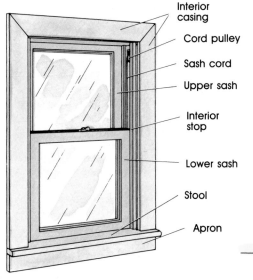

1. Remove interior casing and inside stops.

2. Raise the lower sash and tap or pry the stool up. Then move to the outside.

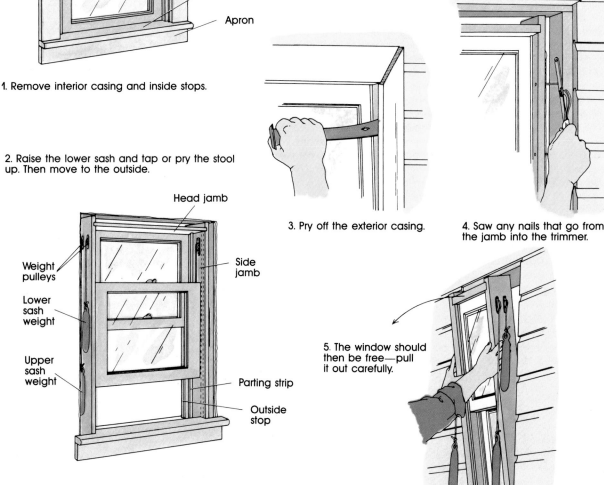

3. Pry off the exterior casing.

4. Saw any nails that go from the jamb into the trimmer.

5. The window should then be free—pull it out carefully.

An alternate technique is to disassemble the entire window, taking out the sash first and then the jambs. If the window operates with a sash cord and weights, cut the lower cord and let the weight fall inside the wall. Lift out the lower sash and remove the parting bead that separates the two sashes. Then cut the remaining cord and lift out the upper sash.

If the sashes are spring-loaded, remove the cover from the metal channel. Release the tension from the springs and lift out the lower and then the upper sash. Pull out nails or screws holding the channels in place.

Once the sashes are removed, pry the jambs from the studs or saw them in half and pry out the pieces. Pull out any remaining nails inside the rough opening.

## Installing the New Window

Measure the rough opening to be sure the new window will fit. There should be 1/4- to 1/2-inch clearance all around. To make the opening slightly smaller, nail spacer boards to the sides of the studs. If you're replacing an old-style sash-and-weight window, the rough opening is probably 2 to 2 1/2 inches wider on each side. The extra space accommodated the balance weights inside the wall. Nail new studs or spacer blocks inside the opening to create the proper size.

If there's no building paper on the sheathing around the opening, or if it's in poor condition, staple new pieces in place. This minimizes air and moisture penetration once the window is installed.

Check to make sure the existing drip cap is in good condition and wide enough to fit over the new exterior casing. If the new window or opening doesn't have a drip cap, cut and crimp a piece of aluminum flashing to fit. If possible, the flashing should extend 3 to 4 inches under the siding and 1/2 inch beyond the exterior casing. Often you can buy premolded flashing when you pick up the window.

Unless the manufacturer's instructions say otherwise, leave any braces in place until the window is installed. Cut off any protective horns at either side of the frame.

From the outside, position the window in the rough opening and center it between the trimmer studs. Most new prehung windows come with the exterior casing attached. (The procedure for a custom-milled window

## Installing a New Window

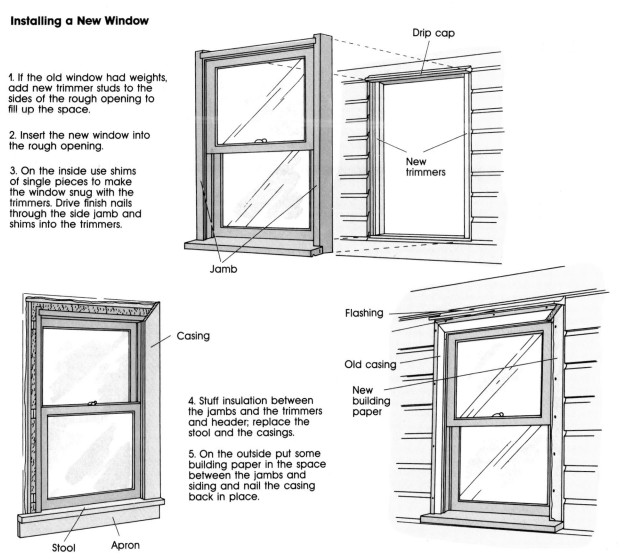

1. If the old window had weights, add new trimmer studs to the sides of the rough opening to fill up the space.

2. Insert the new window into the rough opening.

3. On the inside use shims of single pieces to make the window snug with the trimmers. Drive finish nails through the side jamb and shims into the trimmers.

Jamb

Drip cap

New trimmers

Casing

4. Stuff insulation between the jambs and the trimmers and header; replace the stool and the casings.

5. On the outside put some building paper in the space between the jambs and siding and nail the casing back in place.

Stool     Apron

Flashing

Old casing

New building paper

without the exterior trim is similar except that you secure the window by nailing through the inside jambs. The exterior trim is added later.) The exterior casing should fit snugly against the outside of the sheathing, under the drip cap, and between the edges of the siding.

If the siding needs to be cut, use a circular saw set to the depth of siding and trim the excess away. Make sure you don't cut into the sheathing. Allow ⅛- to ¼-inch clearance on either side. You can fill this with caulking later. Drive a finishing nail through the upper corner of the casing into the header. Level the window and if necessary have a helper on the inside shim under the side jambs. Then drive a second finishing nail through the opposite corner of the casing.

Check the window for plumb by placing a level along the side jamb. Shim at least two places along each jamb. Be careful not to overshim and bow out the jambs. Next check the sashes. If the window wobbles when opened, more shimming is necessary. If the sashes won't open freely, the shims are too tight. Make sure the space between the sash and the frame remains the same when the window is opened and closed.

Once the window is level and plumb with enough shims in place, secure the position by driving finishing nails through the sides of the exterior casing at 10-inch intervals. Countersink the nail heads and fill with wood putty. Caulk completely around the window between the exterior casing, drip cap, and siding. On the inside, add insulation between the window and the studs. It's also a good idea to cover it with a plastic vapor barrier. Reinstall the old interior trim or add new.

### Cutting a Wall for a New Window

To add a new window where none exists, you must cut into the exterior wall and frame a new opening. Follow the same procedure for removing a window and replacing it with a larger size.

Locating the new window depends on preference and the present openings. As a rule the tops of windows and doors are 6 feet 8 inches above the finish floor, but this varies with the age and style of the house. Consistency is the key, especially on the exterior. If the new window is the same size as the old, align it with the top of the existing windows. If the size or style is different, position the window carefully so the harmony of the exterior isn't disrupted. Positioning the window next to an existing stud simplifies the framing, but this isn't essential.

In planning a new window, consider safety requirements such as the need to use safety glass for any window within 18 inches of the floor, to protect toddlers. (Some codes require safety glass in all installations.) Also, overall size may influence thickness of the glass, and therefore, the cost.

You should have the new unit on hand for measuring before you cut the rough opening. If you have any questions or aren't completely sure of the size, be sure to check with the dealer first.

An interior wall surface is generally easier to cut and patch than exterior siding, so start from the inside. Mark the outline of the rough opening on the wall and

### Cutting an Opening for a New Window

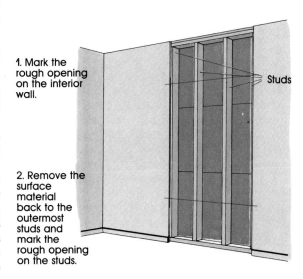

1. Mark the rough opening on the interior wall.

Studs

2. Remove the surface material back to the outermost studs and mark the rough opening on the studs.

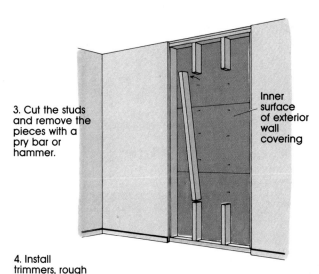

3. Cut the studs and remove the pieces with a pry bar or hammer.

Inner surface of exterior wall covering

4. Install trimmers, rough sill, header, and cripple studs.

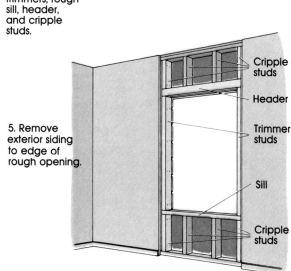

Cripple studs

Header

Trimmer studs

5. Remove exterior siding to edge of rough opening.

Sill

Cripple studs

locate the two studs on the outer edges. *Be sure to turn off any electrical circuits in the vicinity before you begin cutting.* Remove the insulation from the space and re-route any electrical wiring. Then cut and strip the surface between the studs.

If the ceiling joists run perpendicular to the wall, erect a temporary support to carry the bearing load (see page 42). If the ceiling joists run parallel to the wall, supports aren't necessary.

Next prepare a header of sufficient size to carry the weight of the wall and any other loads once the studs are cut. For openings up to 4 feet wide supporting only the roof, the header generally should be a 4 by 4. For openings up to 5 feet wide, the header should be a 4 by 6. But this depends on the location of the window and the weight the header must support. Check the local code to determine the exact size required. The header can be solid wood or built up from 2-by lumber with plywood spacers in between. The width of the header should be slightly less than the width of the studs. If the studs are 3½ inches wide, use ³/₈-inch plywood for spacers. In an older home the studs may be wider than this, so ½-inch plywood can be used. Nail the header together on both sides with 16d nails staggered along its length about every 12 inches.

Mark one of the studs inside the opening with the desired height of the window. Add a second mark above this that includes the depth of the header plus ¼ inch for clearance. Use a square to mark each stud and then cut with a backsaw or reciprocating saw. To determine the lower cut, add the depth of the rough opening, plus 1½ inches for a new 2-by-4 rough sill, plus ¼ inch for clearance. Mark and cut the studs; then remove the pieces from the opening. Use a pry bar or hit the side of the stud with a hammer to loosen from the sheathing.

If one or two new full-length studs are necessary, toenail them to the top and sole plates. Otherwise use the existing studs at the outer edges of the opening. Cut two trimmer studs to fit between the sole plate and header. Use a plumb bob or level to be sure they're plumb; then nail to the full-length studs with 10d nails every 12 inches. Position the header over the trimmers and check for level. Drive three or four 16d nails through each full-length stud into the end of the header. Then toenail the header to the trimmer studs and to the cripple studs overhead. If necessary, shim between the cripples and the header for a snug fit. Cut and install the rough sill by nailing it to the cripples underneath. Shim as necessary to make the sill level. At this point the rough opening is complete, and you can remove any temporary supports.

**An alternate technique.** Instead of marking and cutting the studs inside the opening, remove them completely. Cut the trimmers from the salvaged studs; then install the trimmers and header as described previously. Cut the necessary cripples and toenail in place. Finally add the rough sill.

**A second alternative.** Removing the wall surface beyond the exact size of the rough opening, as just described, simplifies the framing process. But this also means the wall must be patched once the window is installed. If you're experienced with this type of framing problem, you may choose to cut the opening closer to the exact size and thus eliminate much of the patching. The difficulties with this approach are in cutting the wall material precisely without damage, and in securing the trimmer studs inside a narrow wall cavity.

## Installing Sliding Glass Doors

Sliding glass doors are essentially oversize windows large enough to walk through. Two-panel units are most common—one door slides and the other remains stationary. Triple panels are also available. Standard widths range from 5 to 8 feet, and the usual height is 80 to 82 inches. Most doors are preglazed; otherwise the glass is added after the doors are in place.

Selection and installation procedures are similar to those for a prehung window. Like new windows, sliding glass doors are available in wood, metal, and vinyl-clad wood. Choose a style that's compatible with the rest of the house. You should also consider the amount of maintenance involved.

The larger the opening, the more it jeopardizes the wall's shear strength. Adding plywood panels on both sides of the new door increases shear strength. For energy savings compare different models and investigate the types of weatherstripping and thermal barriers available. Since the glass area is so large, double-pane insulating glass is highly recommended. If small children may be in the house, also consider the benefits of safety glass. Accidents happen all too easily. For safety's sake view the additional cost as an inexpensive insurance policy.

Installing a new sliding glass door is not that difficult since much of the frame and hardware are pre-assembled by the manufacturer. The major task is preparing the rough opening. For that you can refer to the previous section on adding a new window (see page 71), with one precaution: when installing a large slider in a wall supporting a second story, be careful to size the header properly and shore the ceiling during installation. The process of cutting and framing the opening differs in only a few ways.

### Preparing the Rough Opening for a Sliding Glass Door

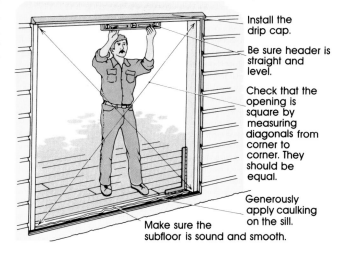

Install the drip cap.

Be sure header is straight and level.

Check that the opening is square by measuring diagonals from corner to corner. They should be equal.

Generously apply caulking on the sill.

Make sure the subfloor is sound and smooth.

■ It's critical that the rough opening be square and plumb. If it isn't, the frame may not fit or the door may not slide or latch properly. Measure diagonally to check.
■ The subfloor should be sound and smooth. After you remove the sole plate, you may need to add a filler board to bring the subfloor to the proper depth. Slight irregularities can be planed or sanded smooth.
■ If there is a slight bow in the header material, be sure to install the crown or high side to the top.
■ Install the drip cap before the frame.

If the door frame isn't assembled, set it up according to the directions provided by the manufacturer. Apply a generous amount of caulking to the bottom of the sill. Paper flashing is also advised. Working from the outside, position the frame in the rough opening. Take care not to twist the frame out of shape. It's advisable to have a helper to hold the frame in place. Otherwise secure it temporarily by driving finishing nails through the exterior casing into the trimmer studs. If the frame has no casing, use C-clamps to hold it against the sheathing.

Press down along the length of the sill to spread the caulking. This will create a tight seal between the frame and the subfloor. To ensure trouble-free operation, the sill must be level. If it isn't, shim as necessary. Then screw the inner edge of the sill to the subfloor every 10 to 12 inches. If the floor is concrete, drill holes for expansion shields and anchor the sill with screws.

Check the side jambs for plumb. At the location of each predrilled hole in the frame, shim between the jambs and the trimmer studs. Make sure you don't over-shim and bow the jambs. Drill pilot holes and drive wood screws through the jambs and shims into the trimmer studs. Follow the same procedure for the top jamb. Tighten the screws snugly but don't pull the jambs out of shape. If you do, the door won't seal or slide smoothly.

For a frame with exterior casing attached, drive finishing nails through the casing into the trimmer studs and header at 10- to 12-inch intervals. If the manufacturer has provided a sill support, place it under the sill overhang and secure to the exterior sheathing with screws or finishing nails. Otherwise cut a 1-inch wood support the length of the sill and nail it in place.

Position the stationary panel in the outer channel of the frame. To get the right position, align the predrilled screw holes. Next secure the panel to the frame. This depends on the type of door and the manufacturer. Most panels are anchored with one or two brackets in the top and bottom rails, plus security screws through the parting strip that separates the stationary and sliding panels.

Next install the sliding panel. Tip the panel at the top and slide it along the channel to the closed position. Secure the door in the track according to the manufacturer's directions. Slide the door back and forth to check its operation. If it sticks or binds or isn't square with the frame, locate the adjustment screws and raise or lower the door. If the frame requires a threshold, fasten it to the floor with screws. Add insulation between the frame and the studs; then patch the wall with wallboard or trim with molding. Finally patch any cavities left in the finish floor with new flooring material.

## Installing Sliding Glass Doors

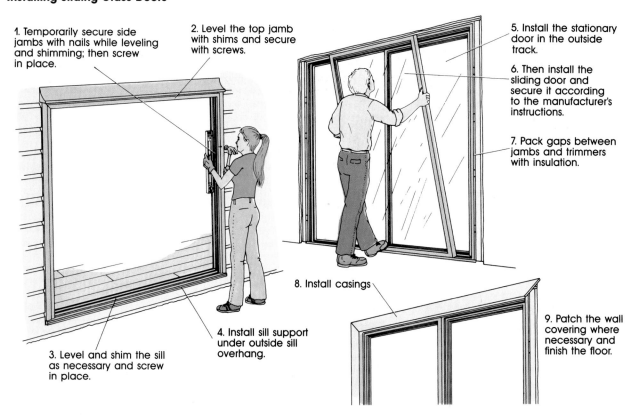

1. Temporarily secure side jambs with nails while leveling and shimming; then screw in place.

2. Level the top jamb with shims and secure with screws.

3. Level and shim the sill as necessary and screw in place.

4. Install sill support under outside sill overhang.

5. Install the stationary door in the outside track.

6. Then install the sliding door and secure it according to the manufacturer's instructions.

7. Pack gaps between jambs and trimmers with insulation.

8. Install casings

9. Patch the wall covering where necessary and finish the floor.

# ADDING A SKYLIGHT

In many areas of the country, adding a skylight to your home can have several benefits. The most obvious, of course, is an abundance of natural light. Skylights transmit up to five times more light per square foot than conventional wall windows. The switch from artificial lighting can transform dark inner areas of the house.

Although flat sheets of acrylic plastic are sometimes used to custom build a skylight, it's difficult to achieve a permanent weathertight seal because of expansion and contraction. A better choice is to buy a prefabricated skylight made of acrylic or glass. These units are easier to install and, if sealed properly, less likely to leak. They also have interior gutters to catch and remove condensation drips. Some are self-flashing; others require flashing added during installation. If glass is used, the building code generally specifies wire mesh or tempered glass with wire screening, although laminated safety plate is acceptable in many areas.

Most prefabricated skylights are constructed with two domes or panes, either clear or tinted. A thermal insulation barrier between the two minimizes the transfer of heat or cold through the skylight surface. If both glazings are clear, the sky and and sun are visible from inside the house. If the inner dome is translucent (white or tinted), the incoming light is distributed more evenly without glare. Rain streaks and debris such as twigs and leaves are also less noticeable. If additional ventilation is important, choose a style that opens and closes.

Skylights are sized to fit between standard rafter openings. The smallest, 14½ inches wide, nests snugly between rafters 16 inches on center. Other modular sizes, such as 32 and 48 inches, require cutting one or two rafters. Thus, the existing rafter spacing in your house is a major factor in determining the proper size skylight.

A second factor to consider is the following rule of thumb: the ratio between the skylight opening and the covered floor space is approximately 1:20. This means that a 4-square-foot skylight (24 by 24 inches) provides adequate lighting for 80 square feet of floor area; an 8-square-foot unit (24 by 48 inches) accommodates 160 square feet.

## Preparing the Rough Opening

To cut into the roof, begin from the inside and mark the proposed opening on the sheathing between existing rafters. If the rafters are covered, first strip the ceiling surface (see page 36). Because new headers must be added between the rafters, be sure to add 1½ inches to the top and bottom edges of the opening. The header size should be the same as the rafters. (If only one rafter needs to be cut, single headers of 2-by lumber are generally sufficient. If you're cutting two rafters, however, the headers may need to be doubled. The rafters themselves may also need to be doubled on either side of the opening, in which case the ceiling material must be removed along the length of the rafters. This depends primarily on the snow load in your area, so ask the building department for advice.) At each corner of the opening, drive 16d nails or drill guide holes through the roof.

**Preparing the Rough Opening for a Skylight**

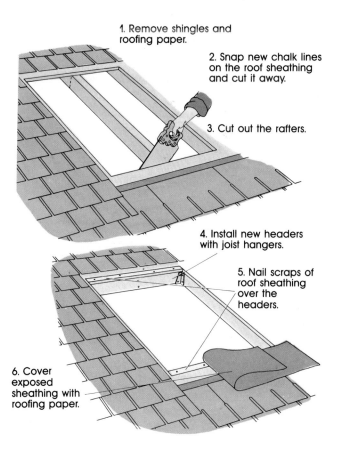

1. Remove shingles and roofing paper.

2. Snap new chalk lines on the roof sheathing and cut it away.

3. Cut out the rafters.

4. Install new headers with joist hangers.

5. Nail scraps of roof sheathing over the headers.

6. Cover exposed sheathing with roofing paper.

## Working on the Roof

Take great care whenever you go up on a roof. A broken limb will slow down more than your remodeling. If you have any doubts about working high above the ground, leave this job to someone else. Plan to take these or similar precautions.

■ Wear shoes with flexible rubber soles for a better grip.

■ Don't go on the roof when it's damp from rain, dew, or frost.

■ Stay well away from power lines.

■ For secure footing, buy or rent safety hooks. These clamp over the ridge and secure an extension ladder to the roof surface.

■ Along the side of the house, use a rented metal scaffold. This provides a level work surface and minimizes damage to the roof and gutters. Erect the scaffold on 2-by-6 planks and follow the assembly instructions provided by the rental outlet. In some cases the rental fee includes their installation. The better scaffolds have a guard rail at the top level.

■ Nail a large tarp or roll of heavy plastic to the ridge in case of bad weather. Once the roof is cut, the work should proceed without interruption or delay until the skylight is framed and made weathertight.

On the roof, double check the dimensions because you may not have driven the nails straight through. Snap chalk lines to connect the corners and outline the opening. Next remove the shingles inside the lines, plus enough extra around the edges to install the curb. Exactly how much has to be removed depends on the type of skylight. If the unit is self-flashing, follow the manufacturer's recommendations for stripping the roof. In some cases this may be 12 to 16 inches beyond the rough opening. If the unit is without flashing and the roofing is asphalt shingles, cut an extra 1½ to 2 inches outside the chalk lines at the top and sides. This is generally sufficient for slipping new flashing under the shingles. With wood shingles or shakes, you should remove an extra 8 inches all around.

Asphalt shingles can be cut with a utility or shingling knife. Lift the shingles and remove the exposed nails with a pry bar. If the shingles are bonded together with roofing cement or self-sealing tabs, use a stiff putty knife to separate them. To remove shingles that have been nailed twice with the upper row of nails hidden, cut or rip out several shingles at the top of the opening. Then, once the nails are exposed, work your way down. If the manufacturer recommends stripping beyond the rough opening, work carefully so as not to damage shingles that don't need to be removed. Those removed will need to be replaced with new shingles later.

With wood shakes or shingles, use a utility knife to split the upper row and pull out the pieces. Then work downward, removing the exposed nails with a pry bar. To cut hidden nails, slip a hacksaw blade underneath. In some cases it may be easier to start at the peak of the roof and remove a section of the roofing all the way down to the opening.

Once the roofing material is removed, use a utility knife to cut away the building paper. Snap new chalk lines on the sheathing and cut through it with a reciprocating or circular saw. Pry the pieces from the rafters.

With a square, mark the intervening rafters that need to be removed and cut them with a reciprocating or handsaw. Cut two headers to fit between the rafters and secure them with joist hangers. Also nail the headers to the ends of the cut rafters. Nail the new strips of sheathing (cut from the removed sections) over the tops of the headers. Cover with new building paper.

You could install the headers and any trimmers needed to double up rafters before cutting the roof opening. This is a good procedure when threatening weather reduces the time you want to have the roof opened up.

## Installing the Skylight
If the skylight requires a curb, build a 2-by-4 or 2-by-6-inch frame with the inside the size of the rough opening. Set the skylight over the curb and check for fit. If the skylight is not self-flashing, have top and bottom collars made up by a sheet metal shop, as well as step flashing for both sides, ready for installation.

Set the curb on the rough opening so the inside is flush with the sheathing. Toenail the curb in place. Next, with asphalt shingles, use a hacksaw blade to cut away any nails securing the shingles within 4 or 5 inches of the rough opening. Then nail the bottom collar against the curb so it laps over the top of the second row of shingles below the skylight opening. When the shingles just below the skylight are replaced, they go over the collar.

Nail the top corners in place with galvanized roofing nails. Next tuck a piece of step flashing between each course of shingles on both sides of the curb, starting at the bottom. Nail the uphill corners of each step flashing to the curb and into the shingles. Finally, install the top collar so its wings overlap the shingles downslope from it, but its top tucks under the upper course of shingles. Finish by placing the final course of shingles over the collar, tucking each one under the course above it. Next apply strips of foam weatherstripping or a bead of clear mastic to the top of the curb. Then fit the skylight over the curb and tap down. Drill pilot holes for

**Installing the Skylight**

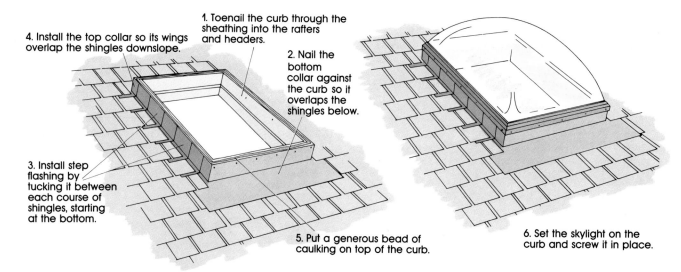

4. Install the top collar so its wings overlap the shingles downslope.

1. Toenail the curb through the sheathing into the rafters and headers.

2. Nail the bottom collar against the curb so it overlaps the shingles below.

3. Install step flashing by tucking it between each course of shingles, starting at the bottom.

5. Put a generous bead of caulking on top of the curb.

6. Set the skylight on the curb and screw it in place.

screws or special nails with neoprene gaskets and secure the flanges all around the curb. Renail the shingles
around the edges of the opening but don't nail through
the bottoms of the flashing. Apply roofing cement to any
exposed nail heads.

If the skylight requires no curb, apply a layer of
roofing cement around the opening. Position the skylight
and screw the unit to the sheathing and rafters according to the manufacturer's instructions. Apply roofing cement along the edges up to the unit. Cut strips of building
paper and place the bottom piece first. Apply cement
over the corners and then add the side pieces. Follow
the same procedure for fitting the top strip. Apply more
cement over the paper and replace the shingles up to
the edge of the skylight.

If you need to build a light shaft, it can be straight,
angled, or flared. The flared design is preferred because it maximizes the distribution of light. The construction is essentially the same for all three; the only difference is in marking the opening and framing.

To build a straight shaft, drop a plumb bob from the
four corners of the skylight. Mark the opening on the
joists and then follow the procedure on page 63 for cutting and framing a stairway opening. For an angled or
flared shaft, cut a larger opening into the ceiling. The
sides of the opening are in line with the sides of the
skylight to avoid breaking extra joists, but the other two
sides are flared. Enclose the shaft with short 2-by-4 walls
complete with top and sole plates. Insulate between the
studs with fiberglass batts, facing the vapor barrier toward the inside of the shaft. Finish with wallboard and
paint white or a bright color to reflect the incoming light.

A final touch is to provide movable insulation for
covering the skylight at night. A shutter can be im-
provised by covering a piece of rigid foam or fiberglass
board with attractive fabric. Attach it to the skylight
opening with hinges and rig a pull string. A 3-inch thick
shutter can have an R-value of 19, versus 5 or 6 for a
triple-glazed skylight unit.

### Light Shaft Variations

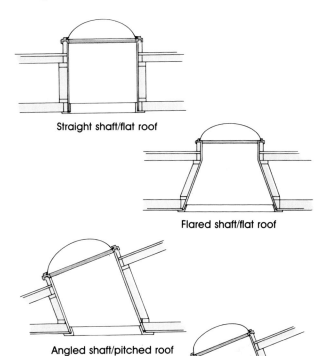

Straight shaft/flat roof

Flared shaft/flat roof

Angled shaft/pitched roof

Flared shaft/pitched roof

### Building a Light Shaft

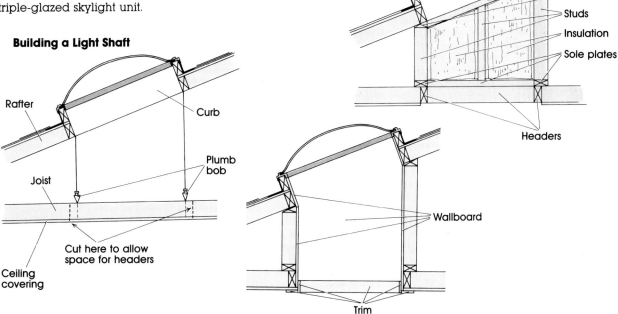

Rafter

Curb

Plumb
bob

Joist

Cut here to allow
space for headers

Ceiling
covering

Top plates

Studs

Insulation

Sole plates

Headers

Wallboard

Trim

# BUILDING A DORMER

Building a dormer can convert a small, dark attic into a bright and spacious living area. Adding one or more windows improves light and ventilation. The usable floor space is also significantly increased. Depending on the exact size and shape of the dormer, the increase may be as much as 30 to 40 percent. If you compare the cost to a complete addition, a new dormer is an appealing project indeed.

## Planning the Project

But adding a dormer also demands careful planning and skillful carpentry. In many instances you would be wise to seek professional assistance. If you have relatively little building experience, think seriously about hiring a contractor for at least part of the job. Perhaps you can work alongside and learn as you go. Or have the contractor handle the more difficult aspects such as cutting into the roof and framing the shell. Then finish the job yourself, employing many of the techniques described in other sections of this book.

There are also compelling reasons for consulting a designer at the outset of the project. First the dormer size should be planned carefully to maximize the available living space. The optimum size reflects a delicate balance between your needs and your budget. A designer can help you get the most for your improvement dollars.

Second since the addition will dramatically alter the exterior appearance of the house, good design is essential. The dormer should match the style of the existing architecture. Generally the same type of windows, siding, and roofing should be used, and any details such as overhangs and fascia should be repeated. Most important, the dormer should blend smoothly with the rest of the house, complementing the overall design. In fact, the dormer shouldn't appear to be an addition at all, but part of the original construction. If the proportion or location is wrong, the dormer will always look tacked on.

Dormers take two basic shapes: gable and shed. The *gable dormer* is generally smaller, adding light but

not much floor space. It's also more difficult to build since it requires joining two sloping surfaces into the existing roofline. Often two or more gable dormers are necessary to balance the exterior proportions of the house.

The *shed dormer* has a single sloping roofline that connects with the house at the ridge beam or farther down the slope of the roof. The front of the dormer can rest directly over the exterior wall below, or be set back several feet. The latter design generally results in a more attractive exterior appearance.

The advantages of the shed dormer are twofold: it's easier to build, and it adds more usable living space with maximum headroom. This section shows how to frame and enclose a shed dormer that's set back from the ridge and eave. The framing is basically the same for a ridge-to-eave dormer; only the details in connecting to the house are different.

To plan the new dormer, begin by determining the slope of the existing roof. To do this you must be familiar with some basic roofing terminology. The *span* is the width of the house and the *run* is half the width. The *rise* is the vertical distance between the cap plate and the ridge beam. The *slope* expresses the ratio between the rise and the run. For example, if the rise of your roof is 10 feet and the run is 20 feet, the ratio is 10 to 20, but the slope is expressed as 6 in 12, which means the roof rises 6 inches for 12 inches of run.

You can use either of two techniques to find the slope of the roof. The first is to measure the actual rise and span of the house. The second and easier method is to mark off 12 inches along the top of a carpenter's level. Position one end of the level against a rafter; then measure the rise at the 12-inch mark. For example, if the rise is 8 inches, the slope is 8 in 12. Choose a straight rafter.

Next use the span and the slope to draw an accurate end view of the roof and attic on ¼-inch graph paper. If the attic is unfinished, determine the desirable ceiling height (see page 58). Sketch the approximate shape of the dormer along the side elevation of the

**Gable Dormer**

**Shed Dormer**

house. For a flat ceiling, plan to add ceiling joists. For a sloping ceiling, the slope of the dormer rafters determines the slope of the ceiling.

Besides considerations of exterior appearance and usable interior space, the possible size and shape of the new dormer are affected by a third factor—the roofing material. Check the building code for the minimum slope allowed for various types of roofing. These requirements vary depending on the climate, especially in locations with heavy rain or snow loads. As a rule the minimum slope for wood shingles and shakes is 4 in 12. For asphalt shingles the slope must be at least 3 in 12, although some codes allow a lower slope if the shingles are self-sealing and the underlayment of building paper is doubled. For roll roofing the slope can be as low as 1 in 12. If the dormer is to the rear of the house, you may decide that roll roofing, although generally unattractive, is satisfactory. If it's high enough, the roof may not be visible from the ground. If the dormer faces the street, however, you should match the roofing on the rest of the house.

## Installing the Dormer

Once you've worked out a satisfactory plan, you're ready to begin the actual construction of your new dormer. If the attic is unfinished, you will probably need to reinforce the floor system by adding new joists between the old (see page 59). Then nail down a ⁵/₈-inch plywood subfloor to provide a sound work surface for the rest of the job (see page 60).

Begin from inside the attic by doubling the rafters on either side of the proposed opening. The new rafters should be the same size as the old and extend from the ridge board to the cap plate. Use a bevel gauge to mark the angles at both ends. Nail to the existing rafters with 10d nails staggered every 12 inches. Drive three 16d nails through the ridge board into the ends of the new rafters.

Mark the opening along the roof sheathing. At the four corners, drill guide holes or drive 16d nails through the sheathing and roofing. From the outside, using the protruding nails, snap chalk lines to outline the opening. Remove the roofing material following the procedures

### Planning a Shed Dormer

Method 1 of finding the roof slope: Multiply the rise by 12 and divide by the run (e.g., 9⅓ × 12 ÷ 14 = 8). The slope is 8 in 12.

Method 2: Mark off 12″ on a carpenter's level. Hold one end against the rafter and measure vertically at the mark to find the slope.

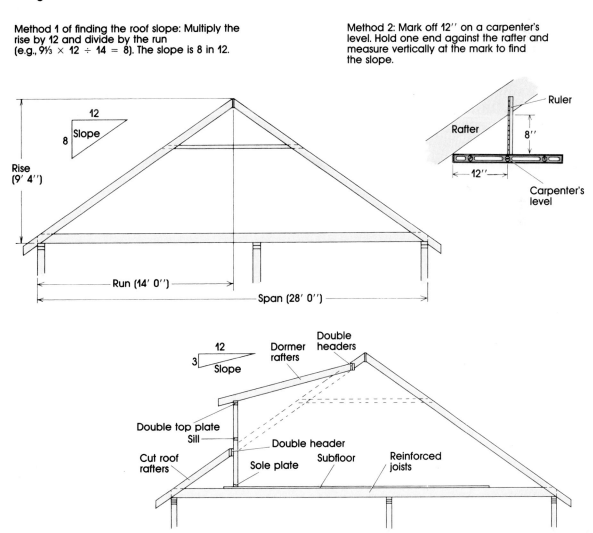

shown on page 77, going beyond the chalk lines 10 to 12 inches. If the roofing is in good condition, salvage as much as you can. It can be reused on the dormer for a perfect match. Otherwise rip it off and remove it from the roof so you don't slip on loose pieces.

Once the roofing material is removed, cut away the building paper with a utility knife. Snap new chalk lines. Set a circular saw or reciprocating saw to the depth of the sheathing and cut along the lines. Pry the pieces carefully from the rafters with a wrecking bar or flat bar. The sheathing can also be reused.

For a set back dormer you should brace the rafters before they are cut. (If there are kneewalls already in place, the lower bracing isn't necessary.) Nail 2 by 4s to

the bottom of the rafters, just above and below the opening. Nail 2-by-4 sole plates to the subfloor; then wedge studs between the two plates under every rafter.

Use a bevel gauge or level to mark the rafters for a plumb cut. Have a helper support the rafter as you cut both ends with a handsaw or reciprocating saw. Remove the cut portions and set them on the subfloor. (Don't drop them, or the ceiling surface downstairs may be jarred loose.) Nail a 3-inch joist hanger to the double rafters at each corner of the opening. Cut a header the same size as the rafters and place in the hanger. Nail through the header into the ends of each cut rafter with two or three 16d nails. Install the second header and face nail to the first with 10d nails every 12 inches in a

## Building a Dormer

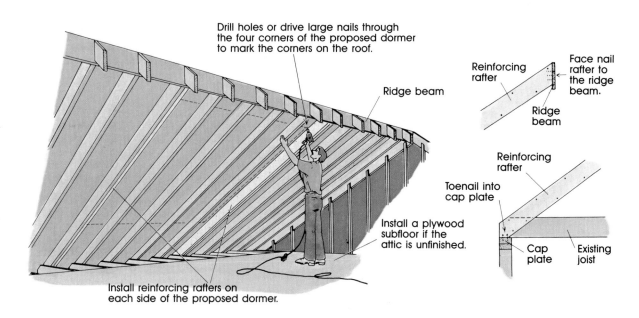

Drill holes or drive large nails through the four corners of the proposed dormer to mark the corners on the roof.

Ridge beam

Face nail rafter to the ridge beam.

Reinforcing rafter

Ridge beam

Reinforcing rafter

Toenail into cap plate

Cap plate

Existing joist

Install a plywood subfloor if the attic is unfinished.

Install reinforcing rafters on each side of the proposed dormer.

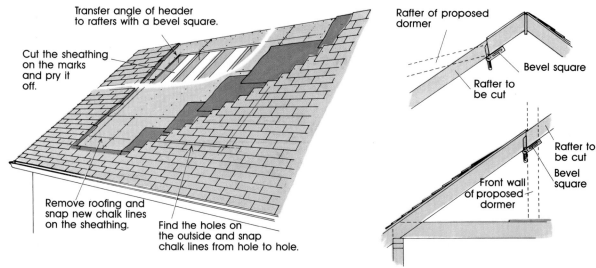

Transfer angle of header to rafters with a bevel square.

Cut the sheathing on the marks and pry it off.

Remove roofing and snap new chalk lines on the sheathing.

Find the holes on the outside and snap chalk lines from hole to hole.

Transfer angles of headers from your drawing to the rafters with a bevel square.

Rafter of proposed dormer

Bevel square

Rafter to be cut

Rafter to be cut

Bevel square

Front wall of proposed dormer

staggered pattern. Install the double headers at the bottom of the opening in the same way. With this done you can remove the temporary bracing.

Frame the front wall for the dormer on the floor of the attic, following the procedures shown on page 50. To frame the window opening, see page 71. The length of the wall is the distance between the double rafters. But in this instance make the top plate long enough to extend beyond the end studs 3½ inches on each side. Stand the framework in place. Brace temporarily with a diagonal 2 by 4 tacked to a block nailed to the subfloor. After plumbing the wall, nail through the sole plate into the joists. Toenail the studs to the header and face nail the end studs to the double rafters.

Build corner posts for the wall with two 2 by 4s and scraps of ⅜-inch plywood in between. The height of the posts extends from the roof sheathing at the corner of the opening to the top plate. Cut the bottom of the posts at the angle of the roofline. (Use the bevel gauge or stand the post against the rafter and mark the angle with a pencil.) Plumb the posts and toenail through the sheathing into the rafters below. Then nail the end studs of the front wall and the top plate to the posts. Nail a cap plate over the length of the wall.

You're now ready to fit and install the rafters. These should be the same size and spacing as the house rafters. (Use the cut rafters if they're long enough. If you use new lumber, be sure to place the crown, or high side, up.)

## Building a Dormer (Continued)

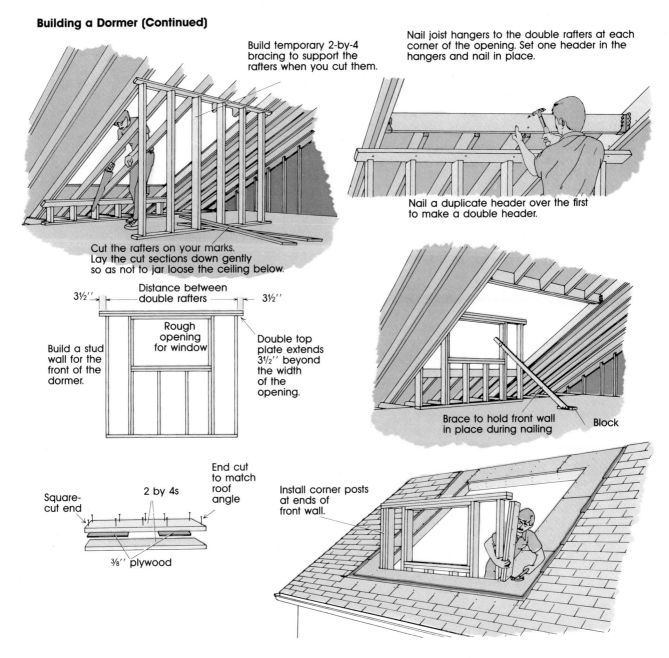

Build temporary 2-by-4 bracing to support the rafters when you cut them.

Cut the rafters on your marks. Lay the cut sections down gently so as not to jar loose the ceiling below.

Build a stud wall for the front of the dormer.

3½″ — Distance between double rafters — 3½″

Rough opening for window

Double top plate extends 3½″ beyond the width of the opening.

Square-cut end

2 by 4s

End cut to match roof angle

⅜″ plywood

Nail joist hangers to the double rafters at each corner of the opening. Set one header in the hangers and nail in place.

Nail a duplicate header over the first to make a double header.

Brace to hold front wall in place during nailing

Block

Install corner posts at ends of front wall.

Mark the correct spacing along the cap plate and header.

To mark the plumb cut at the end of the rafters, either of the techniques can be used. If you know the exact slope of the dormer roof, use the framing square to mark off the rise on the tongue and the run on the blade. Drawing a pencil along the edge of the tongue gives you the cutting angle. If this isn't possible, have a helper hold the end of the rafter so the bottom edge aligns with the inner edge of the cap plate. At the other end hold a piece of scrap wood along the top of the rafter until it connects with the header. Position a level against the rafter next to the header; then mark along the side with a pencil. Cut the rafter and check it for fit.

If the plan calls for the rafters to overhang the front wall of the dormer, reposition the rafter as before and mark the outer end for a *birdsmouth*—a notch cut into the rafter to provide a level surface for the rafter to rest or bear on a wall. If there's no overhang, mark the rafter for a heel cut along the bottom and plumb cut at the front edge. Once the first rafter is properly cut, use it as a template for cutting all the other inside rafters.

The outside rafters will be placed over the double rafters instead of against the header. Thus the end angle is different. To determine this angle, place one end of the trimmer rafter alongside the double rafters, with the upper end against the header and the lower end on the cap plate. Then mark the side of the rafter by drawing a pencil along the edge of the sheathing. Transfer this angle and make the cut.

To install the rafters, secure their top ends to the header with joist hangers. Toenail their lower ends to the cap plate or use framing anchors. For the outer rafters, drive 16d nails through the bottom edge into the double rafters.

With the rafters in place, frame the gable ends of the shed. Mark a sole plate to fit between the corner post and the outside rafter. Bevel the ends for a snug fit. Nail through the sheathing into the double rafters with 16d nails. Mark stud locations along the sole plate, 16 inches on center. Hold each 2-by-4 stud vertically in its place with a level and mark where it touches the rafter. The top of the stud can be notched to accept the outside rafter or cut at an angle.

If the plan calls for ceiling joists, install these as shown on page 62. Sheath the exterior walls as shown on page 86. You can sheath the roof with salvaged materials or use new 1/2-inch sheathing grade plywood or 1-by-4 boards. Apply new shingles, being sure to flash the seams between roof and sidewall or roof and chimney with step flashing.

At this point the exterior of the dormer is ready for finishing with roofing and siding. (Information on selecting and installing various types of roofing and siding is covered in Ortho's book *Basic Carpentry Techniques.*) To complete the interior framing of the attic, see page 61.

## Building a Dormer (Continued)

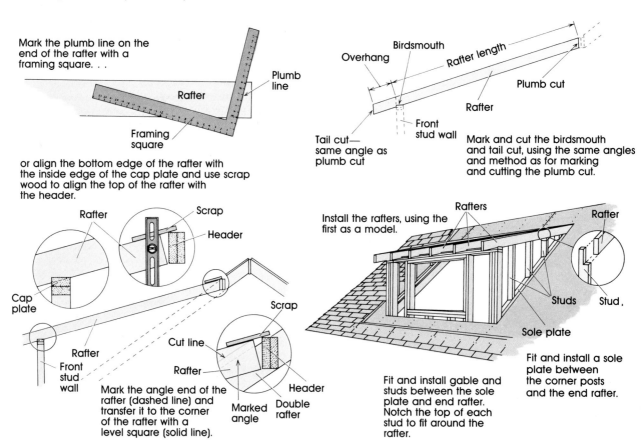

Mark the plumb line on the end of the rafter with a framing square. . .

Plumb line

Rafter

Framing square

or align the bottom edge of the rafter with the inside edge of the cap plate and use scrap wood to align the top of the rafter with the header.

Rafter    Scrap    Header

Cap plate

Rafter
Front stud wall

Mark the angle end of the rafter (dashed line) and transfer it to the corner of the rafter with a level square (solid line).

Cut line    Scrap
Rafter    Header
Marked angle    Double rafter

Overhang    Birdsmouth    Rafter length    Plumb cut    Rafter

Tail cut— same angle as plumb cut    Front stud wall

Mark and cut the birdsmouth and tail cut, using the same angles and method as for marking and cutting the plumb cut.

Install the rafters, using the first as a model.

Rafters    Rafter

Studs    Stud

Sole plate

Fit and install gable and studs between the sole plate and end rafter. Notch the top of each stud to fit around the rafter.

Fit and install a sole plate between the corner posts and the end rafter.

# CONVERTING A GARAGE

Converting a garage provides an easy means of gaining new living space. In most cases the space is dry, well ventilated, and completely weatherized. The floor is solid and the walls are generally ready for finishing with wallboard or paneling. In short, the typical garage offers 200 to 500 square feet of first-class real estate just waiting for improvement.

Before you charge ahead, however, check the building code for restrictions that may apply. In some areas the code specifies that each home must have enclosed off-street parking. If this is the case, you can't legally convert the garage to living space.

The code may require additional windows, especially if the space will be used for sleeping. If you need to add windows, see page 71. To add a conventional door or sliding glass doors, see page 48 or 75.

One of the first problems you'll face is the driveway leading to the garage. Often it's desirable to leave the slab in place and use the driveway for parking. You can build planter boxes between the house and driveway to camouflage the division. Or you can remove the driveway by breaking up the asphalt or concrete surface and removing the pieces. Use a sledgehammer and pick ax or rent an electric jackhammer.

## Replacing the Garage Door
Removing the garage door generally means disassembling the unit in place. Garage doors vary a great deal in how they are assembled. Refer to the installation instuctions if you still have them. Otherwise you may need to call an owner-builder center for specifics on your unit.

Since the door is heavy and the springs can be very dangerous, get help in handling it. If the door is spring-balanced (most are), open it and prop it in place with several 2 by 4s to relieve the tension. Find the bolts or S-hooks that release the tension on the springs and disconnect them carefully. Then remove the props and close the door slowly to keep it from slamming shut. Disassemble the hardware and tracks. If the door is

hinged in several places, take it apart in sections light enough to carry. Use a flat bar to pry the exterior trim from around the door.

With the overhead door and trim removed, frame a new wall to enclose the garage, as shown on page 50. One difference here is that the framework requires no top plate. Simply leave the existing header in place and toenail the studs to the bottom of the header. The sole plate can be nailed to the slab with concrete nails, but lag bolts and expansion shields 24 to 30 inches apart are preferred. Since the sole plate is in contact with masonry, coat it with preservative or use pressure-treated lumber.

Mark the header and plate for the location of new studs 16 inches o.c. (Make sure the positions of the lags and studs don't conflict.) If you plan to add a window, frame the opening as shown on page 73. The window header bears no weight, so use two 2 by 4s laid flat.

To create a termite barrier beneath the sole plate of the new wall, cut a piece of aluminum flashing as long as the sole plate and 7 to 9 inches wide. Bend the flashing at an oblique angle, as shown in the illustration. It works best to bend it over the edge of the board. Apply a bead of caulking to the slab and press the flashing in place. Add more caulking and bolt the sole plate over it to the floor.

Once the frame is complete, cover the exterior with sheathing. Check the existing sheathing on either side of the opening. It's not essential to use the same material, but the new sheathing should match the thickness of the old. Or nail furring strips to the studs to build the proper thickness.

Sheathing grade plywood $1/2$ inch thick goes up fast and provides a solid nailing surface for all types of siding. Apply the panels horizontally with 8d nails spaced 6 inches apart at the edges and 12 inches inside the field. Stagger the joints on different studs. To allow for expansion leave a gap of $1/16$ inch at the ends and $1/8$ inch at the edges. Staple or nail building paper over the plywood, overlapping the paper about 6 inches.

**Framing a New Garage Wall**

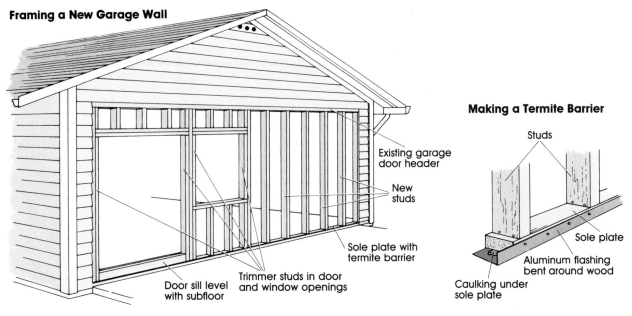

Existing garage door header

New studs

Sole plate with termite barrier

Trimmer studs in door and window openings

Door sill level with subfloor

**Making a Termite Barrier**

Studs

Sole plate

Aluminum flashing bent around wood

Caulking under sole plate

If the siding doesn't require a continuous nailing surface—such as clapboard applications—treated fiberboard sheathing can be used. Panels are generally 2 by 8 feet in size and $1/2$ inch thick. Secure the fiberboard to the studs with 6d roofing nails spaced 3 inches apart at the edges and 6 inches elsewhere.

Solid boards are the least expensive type of sheathing but take more time to install. Apply 1-by-6 or 1-by-8 boards diagonally and nail with two or three 8d nails at each stud. Cover the boards with building paper to minimize air and moisture penetration.

## Finishing the Exterior

To finish the exterior you have three options: (1) remove the old siding surrounding the opening and re-side the entire wall, (2) fill in the space with new material that doesn't match exactly but harmonizes with the old, or (3) patch new pieces of the same type of siding into the material already in place.

If the old wall was a little larger than the doorway itself, the first option is easiest. Remove the old material completely and re-side the wall as in new construction.

The second option is feasible if you are adding new windows that extend across the width of the opening. The only area that needs to be covered is beneath the windows, so use plywood siding or cedar shingles to contrast with the surrounding material. Landscaping under the windows can be used to minimize the difference.

The third option, and usually the most difficult, is patching old and new siding. This is desirable only when the garage door wall is an extension of another wall of the house. It's essential to blend the new pieces carefully; otherwise the joints will always be obvious. This is practical only with certain types of siding, such as cedar shingles or horizontal lap siding.

To pry up a section of lap siding, insert a pry bar underneath at the edge of the opening. If you need to cut a long section, drive several pieces of shim stock under the board to be cut. Slip a hacksaw blade underneath and cut the nails. Mark the piece with a square and make a smooth vertical cut with a backsaw or reciprocating saw. Continue the process all around the opening, cutting every other row and staggering the joints. After the new siding is pieced in and nailed, fill the joints with wood putty or glazing compound.

To patch cedar shingles, cut every other row with a utility knife and pull out the pieces. Unexposed nails can be cut with a hacksaw blade. Nail in new shingles and stagger the joints. The shingles will weather in a year or so to blend with the old. Or, if you can find them, use old shingles salvaged from another project.

## Finishing the Interior

To prepare the garage floor for finishing, refer to the section on basement floors on page 66. With a few exceptions the problems are similar. The basement is generally well below grade, so insulation under the finish floor is optional. But a garage floor is at ground level and subject to greater fluctuations in temperature. For comfort and energy conservation, extra insulation under the floor is advisable in cold climates. In most cases $3^1/2$-inch fiberglass batts or $3/4$-inch rigid panels are sufficient. Check with the building department for the R-values in your area. Prepare a subfloor and place the insulation between the sleepers. The vapor barrier should face toward the inside of the room.

In many attached garages the concrete slab is below the floor level of the rest of the house. This problem can be solved in either of two ways: save the existing step or raise the height of the subfloor. If you need to

### Prying Up Lap Siding

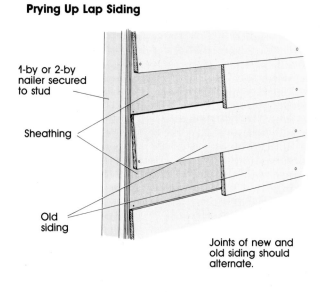

1-by or 2-by nailer secured to stud

Sheathing

Old siding

Joints of new and old siding should alternate.

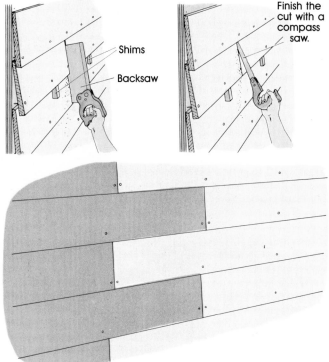

Shims

Backsaw

Finish the cut with a compass saw.

## Constructing a Subfloor on a Concrete Slab

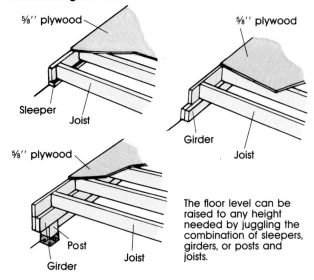

The floor level can be raised to any height needed by juggling the combination of sleepers, girders, or posts and joists.

build a new step because the ceiling height won't allow raising the floor, check the local code first. You may be required to build a landing at least 36 inches square. Construct the framework with 2 by 4s and nail to the subfloor. If steps are necessary, follow the formula for rise and run used in building a stairway.

If you have sufficient headroom in the garage, the subfloor can be raised to any height needed. Simply juggle the combination of sleepers and joists to achieve the right level. For example, 2-by-4 sleepers laid flat, plus 2-by-6 joists set on edge, plus ⅝-inch plywood will raise the height of the floor 7⅝ inches. If the floor must be raised 13 inches, run a 4-by-6 girder (two 2 by 6s nailed together) down the length of the garage. Then span the width with 2-by-8 joists. If the floor must be raised more than this, let's say 18 inches, raise the girder with 4-by-4 posts set in metal supports. Secure the supports to the slab with expansion shields and lag bolts. Other possible combinations include 2-by-3 sleepers, 2 by 4s with 1 by 4s on top, 2-by-10 joists, and so forth.

Depending on the size of the garage, one or two joists will span the width. If 2-by-4 joists are used, place the supporting sleepers every 4 feet; for 2 by 6s, every 6 feet. If two joists are used, overlap them and nail together with 16d nails. Toenail the ends of the joists to the sole plate. If the walls are covered with wallboard, cut away sections to provide access to the plate. If the joists span more than 10 feet, add blocking between them for greater stiffness. Garage slabs are often sloped slightly for better drainage, so shim under the sleepers or joists to level the subfloor. You will need to install a plastic vapor barrier either directly on the slab or between the joists and the subfloor. If you want extra insulation or anticipate moisture problems, put the plastic right under the subfloor.

In most garages the studs are exposed and ready for finishing. Add insulation, a vapor barrier, and ½-inch wallboard. If the walls are already covered with wallboard, probe behind the surface to see if it has been insulated. If not, call several professionals and get bids for blowing in loose fill. If there's no fireblocking in the wall cavities, you may be able to cut notches along the top of the wallboard and pour in the insulation yourself. To create a vapor barrier, paint the wall with two coats of oil enamel, or a sealer followed by a coat of alkyd paint. Another possibility is to remove the existing wallboard, add fiberglass batts, and apply new wallboard. This requires some effort, but the total cost may be lower than that of blowing in loose fill. If you live in a mild climate, the most cost-effective approach may be to leave the walls intact, uninsulated.

If the existing collar beams are at the right height and made of 2-by lumber, use them for finishing the ceiling. Add new ceiling joists as necessary, 16 inches on center. If trusses frame the roof and the span is too great for a single joist, nail strongbacks to the trusses and hang new joists from them.

Insulate between the joists with fiberglass batts, and the ceiling is ready for finishing with wallboard or tile. Don't forget to include a scuttle for access to the newly created attic space.

## Supporting a Long-Span Joist With a Strongback

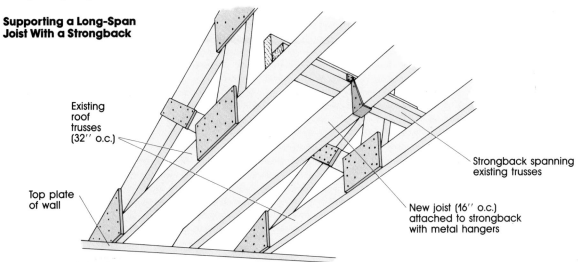

When you still need more room and have exhausted all possibilities for converting unused areas of the house into living space, it's time to consider an add-on. You have three options for expanding your home beyond its present limits: (1) adding out at ground level, (2) adding up with a second floor, or (3) adding down by excavating a basement.

All three types of projects involve extensive new construction, structural modifications to the existing house, design skill in blending the new with the old, and securing proper permits. For detailed instructions on building the foundation, floor framing, wall framing, roof framing, sheathing, siding, and roofing, see Ortho's book *Basic Carpentry Techniques*. For finishing off the addition, see *Basic Carpentry Finishing Techniques*. This section will focus on problems that are unique to joining new and old construction. If you plan to add a new deck or patio, see Ortho's book *How to Design and Build Decks and Patios*.

## Ground-Level Additions

A number of factors enter into planning an addition at ground level.

■ Zoning setback limits can restrict the size or location of the addition.

■ The style of the house requires a compatible addition that either matches or harmonizes with the existing roof line, siding material, window styles, and overall scale.

■ The addition should be located where it's convenient and desirable to open up a wall for access. Ideal situations are existing sliding glass doors or other large windows or a gable wall.

■ The addition should be a shape that encloses the most new space for the given length of wall. Theoretically a circle is the ideal shape, but for practical considerations in building a square is optimum. Forty lineal feet of wall in a rectangular shape does not enclose as much floor space as 40 lineal feet of wall in a square shape. Thus, it may be more practical to add on a square room than to build a long, thin addition across the back of the house.

When these considerations, as well as numerous others like cost, choice of materials, traffic flow, and use of space, are all factored into a final design, you can draw up plans, take out permits, and proceed with the job. For information on building plans and permits, see pages 24 and 25.

This type of addition is quite suitable for a do-it-yourself project. The techniques are common to all new construction and are easy to learn about. The job can stretch out over time because the house is not disturbed by construction debris or weather until the separating wall is actually removed, after the addition is completely closed in. Finally, access and movement of materials are easy since all the work is close to ground level.

**Push-outs.** The simplest type of ground-level addition is to push out the walls with one or more bays. A prefabricated window unit makes the task even simpler. All you do is make a rough window opening in the exterior wall and frame it with new trimmer studs and a properly sized header. Then attach the new window unit to the

### Adding a Prefabricated Window

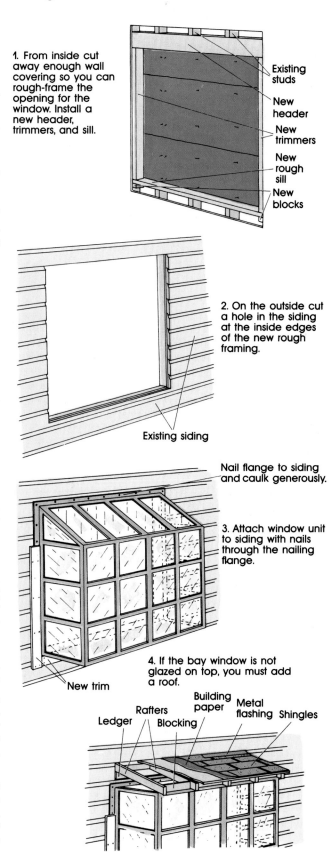

1. From inside cut away enough wall covering so you can rough-frame the opening for the window. Install a new header, trimmers, and sill.

Existing studs

New header

New trimmers

New rough sill

New blocks

2. On the outside cut a hole in the siding at the inside edges of the new rough framing.

Existing siding

Nail flange to siding and caulk generously.

3. Attach window unit to siding with nails through the nailing flange.

New trim

4. If the bay window is not glazed on top, you must add a roof.

Ledger  Rafters  Blocking  Building paper  Metal flashing  Shingles

outside. Caulk the joint between new window and old siding, and cover with new trim boards. The top of the window unit will either be glazed or require roofing, which is a simple matter of building short rafters, attaching sheathing, nailing on shingles, and installing flashing where the new roof joins the side of the house. The inside is finished out with wallboard patching and wood trim. The bottom of the window can either be a plant rack or be modified into a window seat with cushions.

A larger push-out, which still requires no new foundation, can be built by extending the existing floor system with new cantilevered joists, usually 4 to 5 feet out from the house. Start by removing siding and sheathing that cover the existing floor framing along the length of the proposed push-out. Then remove the perimeter joist or rim joist to expose the ends of the floor joists. Nail a new joist of the same depth next to each exposed joist so that no more than one third of its length extends outward to form the cantilevered floor of the new pushout. For example, if the addition extends 4 feet out, install 12-foot joists, with 8 feet doubled against the existing floor joists. Be sure to install blocking between the joists where they cross over the foundation sill or cripple wall, and at the end of the new joists where they are doubled against the

old. Add a header joist at the end of the new joists.

If the existing joists are not perpendicular to the wall, but run parallel, you must cut out sections of five or six of them to be able to run cantilever joists 8 feet back under the floor. The last remaining joist should be doubled, as with a new stairway, and the new cantilever joists anchored to it with metal joist hangers. The cantilever joists now bear 8 feet of the existing floor, as well as the 4-foot push-out. The two outside cantilever joists should be doubled up because they are bearing all the cut ends of the original joists as well as their own loads. This system may require additional support from a new post and pier. Get help in analyzing the floor loads.

Once the floor framing for the push-out is completed, nail down a subfloor and frame up the walls with conventional techniques. Be sure the new framing ties directly into the old. Remove siding and sheathing to expose the old framing. If an existing stud is not available to tie into, add a new stud or entire corner assembly within the cavity of the old wall.

For the roof, either extend the existing roof eave out over the push-out or build a small shed roof that ties into the end wall of the house if the push-out is located on the gable end. The opening between push-out and existing house should be spanned by a properly sized header so that the roof and ceiling loads are still carried directly down to the foundation.

The main advantage of a simple push-out is that it's easy to build. It is not possible with slab foundations or other foundations that lack a wall high enough to cantilever out from. Another limitation is that this type of addition adds very little space, although for enlarging a cramped kitchen or expanding a living room it may be just the solution.

### Extending a Pushout With Cantilevered Joists

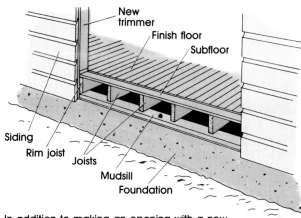

In addition to making an opening with a new header and trimmers, cut the siding and sheathing and remove the rim joist to expose the existing joists.

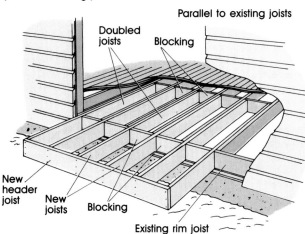

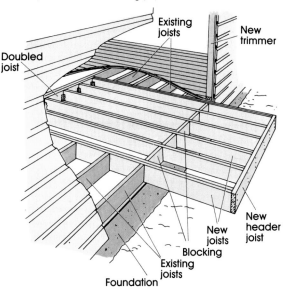

Add new joists, blocking, and header. (Do not cut away the flooring as shown in the drawing; this is for clarity only. Work in the crawl space.)

**Room additions.** The first task in adding a whole room is laying out the perimeter of the new foundation with string lines. Normal batterboards and techniques for squaring the corners are used, except that room additions present one situation that is unique: the house itself may be out of square. If the addition goes on a back corner of the house, where one of its walls becomes an extension of the side wall, it is important that the new foundation and walls be in line with the side of the house, even if that side is not perfectly square with the back of the house. When running the string line for that side of the addition, site along the side of the house and align the string visually, rather than square it a perfect 90 degrees from the back of the house. All other string lines and corners should be square.

Excavation for the new foundation is the same as with new construction, except that it may be impossible to get a backhoe or other large equipment into the backyard. In that case, digging by hand is the only solution. The problem is further compounded by having to remove dirt by wheelbarrow or similar device, unless it can be left in the backyard. In any event you must dig trenches for the foundation footings, and may need to remove some topsoil if a crawl space is required.

The foundation for a room addition involves straightforward techniques for building forms, setting rebar, placing concrete, curing concrete, and stripping forms. The complexity of the job will vary with the style of foundation, slope of the grade, accessibility, and overall size. The style of the foundation is generally the same as that of the house in order to maintain uniform floor levels. The following points are important to consider when joining a new foundation to an old.

■ The new foundation must be physically tied to the old, usually with expansion bolts or rebar set into holes drilled into the old foundation. Use a roto hammer and special masonry bit for drilling holes 7 inches deep and 1/2 to 3/4 inch wide, depending on the size of the bolt. Drill every 24 to 36 inches along the edge of a slab. In a cross section of perimeter wall, drill in the three or four locations where rebar is called out in the plan. Blow out the holes with a tire pump or air syringe. Drive in expansion bolts with a maul, or set 14-inch sections of No. 4 rebar into the holes by packing a paste of slightly expansive cement around them.

■ For a slab foundation be sure to set all plumbing lines in place and wrap with a 1/2-inch layer of protective insulation where they will penetrate the slab. Also protect any wood with a shield of metal flashing where concrete may be poured against it.

■ When establishing the height of a perimeter foundation wall, calculate carefully based on the depth of floor joists you will actually use. The dimensions of new lumber may not match the dimensions of old, forcing the new foundation height to be different from the old.

■ For a perimeter foundation enclosing a crawl space,

### Tying a New Foundation to the Old

### Matching Old and New Subflooring

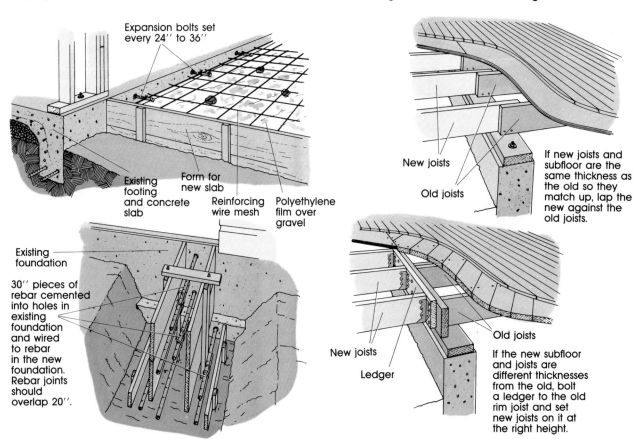

Expansion bolts set every 24″ to 36″

Existing footing and concrete slab

Form for new slab

Reinforcing wire mesh

Polyethylene film over gravel

Existing foundation

30″ pieces of rebar cemented into holes in existing foundation and wired to rebar in the new foundation. Rebar joints should overlap 20″.

New joists

Old joists

If new joists and subfloor are the same thickness as the old so they match up, lap the new against the old joists.

New joists

Ledger

Old joists

If the new subfloor and joists are different thicknesses from the old, bolt a ledger to the old rim joist and set new joists on it at the right height.

you may need to provide an access hole in the new foundation and kneewall, since the new crawl space may be inaccessible from the existing crawl space.

Like the foundation, the floor, wall, and roof framing for a ground-level addition are also straightforward except for tying into the existing house framing. Floor joists can be connected by removing the old rim joist and lapping new joists against the exposed ends of the house's joists. If the new subflooring material will not match up with the old, it is better to leave on the rim joist and butt a ledger to it that is one size larger than the new joists. Then attach new joists to it with joist hangers so they are high enough for the new and old subflooring to match up.

As with simple push-out additions, the wall framing must be tied directly into the house's framing. When connecting new framing to the old, strip away only enough sheathing and siding for access to the connection points. Wait until the addition is closed in before removing the rest of the exterior wall material.

Techniques for tying in the roof framing vary with the design. If the addition is on the gable end of the house, the new rafters will be framed parallel to the old, and the point of connection is simply the first pair of new rafters doubled up against the existing rake rafters on the end of the house.

A more complicated connection occurs when the ridge line of the new roof runs perpendicular to the ridge of the existing house. Then the new roof is tied into the slope of the existing roof, usually some distance below its ridge, creating two new valleys. Frame the new roof by cutting a full pair of pattern rafters. Temporarily support them on the far end of the addition so they hold one end of the ridge board in position. Level the ridge board and mark exactly where it intersects the slope of the existing roof. This point is the apex of the inverted V where the new roof intersects the existing roof slope. Mark this V on the existing roofing material with a nail and strip away enough roofing so 2-by-4 plates can be nailed directly onto the sheathing along the path of the V. Drive 16d nails through the 2 by 4 and sheathing into the rafters below.

Cut an angle on the end of the ridge board so it will lie on the apex of the 2-by-4 plates. Make sure it is level. Then use the two pattern rafters at the far end of the addition to mark and cut the rest of the full rafters. Nail the first pair in place, securing one end of the ridge board to them and its other end to the apex of the roof plates. Nail the rest of the full rafters in place toenailing them to the cap plates with three 16d nails and alternately face nailing and toenailing them to the ridge board with 10d nails. Then cut pairs of progressively shorter jack rafters to fit between the ridge board and roof plates. Cut and fit each pair carefully so they maintain the same roof plane established by the full-size rafters. The best way to check is to lay a long straightedge across their tops.

With the rafters in place, nail down the roof sheathing—either ½-inch plywood for composition and most rigid roofing materials, or 1-by-4 slats for wood shingles.

**Tying New and Old Roofs Together**

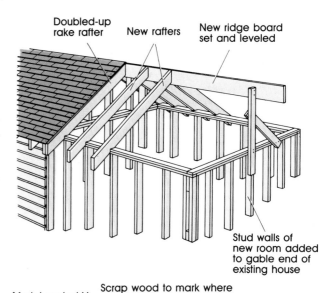

Doubled-up rake rafter — New rafters — New ridge board set and leveled — Stud walls of new room added to gable end of existing house

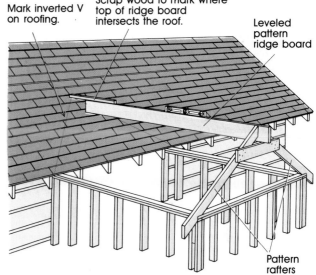

Mark inverted V on roofing. — Scrap wood to mark where top of ridge board intersects the roof. — Leveled pattern ridge board — Pattern rafters

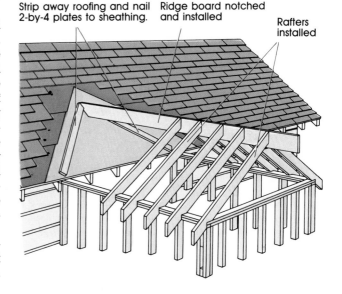

Strip away roofing and nail 2-by-4 plates to sheathing. — Ridge board notched and installed — Rafters installed

## Tying New and Old Roofs Together (Continued)

Line up and install jack rafters with a straight edge laid across other rafters.

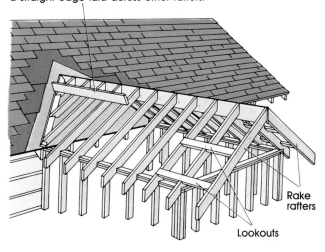

Rake rafters

Lookouts

Nail sheathing to rafters

Add valley flashing or roll roofing depending on valley style.

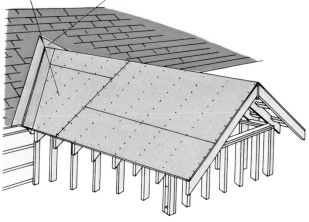

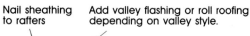

When installing shingles "weave" them one row over the next in the valley.

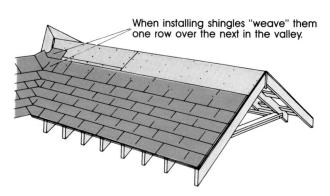

Where it intersects the old roof, cut and nail it so its edge fits snugly against the old sheathing to provide a solid nailing surface, without gaps, along the newly created valleys. Lay plywood perpendicular to the rafters.

Roofing for the new addition must be tied carefully into the old. Choose roofing material that matches the old, unless you are reroofing the entire house. If the new roof is simply an extension of the old gable roof, tie the new roofing material into the old by removing one shingle at the end of every other course of old roofing. Then start the new shingles for each course where the old course ends. That way seams between the old and new will be staggered and not line up in a straight line from eave to ridge.

For roof intersections with one or two new valleys, apply valley flashing first. If the old roof is being reroofed, lay the flashing over the old material. If not, carefully tuck the metal ribbed flashing, or 90-pound roll flashing, under existing shingles all the way up the valley. You will need to remove individual nails first, to make sure the flashing extends the required 8 to 10 inches up under the roofing on each side of the valley. Once the flashing is in place, apply new roofing over it and the rest of the addition.

Siding for the new addition should either match the old or provide a pleasing contrast of texture and color. To make a contrasting material look more harmonious and less "stuck on," it sometimes helps to have the side of the addition set back about 6 inches where it joins the house. (For matching new siding to old, see page 86 on garage conversions.) The new windows should also match the old as much as possible.

The rest of the ground-level addition, such as plumbing, electricity, insulation, and finish trim, uses the same techniques as new construction or basic interior remodeling. When removing part or all of the exterior wall, be sure to install a beam or header of proper size.

### Final Considerations

Each type of room addition has unique advantages and construction problems that must be considered. One more factor, which will ultimately depend on the site orientation and local climate, is energy efficiency. A basement, for instance, shares the advantages of earth-sheltered housing such as superior insulation and modulated temperature swings. A ground-level or second-floor addition can take advantage of any solar exposure simply by having predominantly south-facing glass and a roof slope suitable for mounting solar collectors. In all cases the addition itself can be a sunspace that collects, stores, and distributes solar-generated heat or cooling to the enitre house.

When building room additions, as with all remodeling projects, you should make your home more energy-efficient and structurally sound than it was before. Above all, learn how to enjoy the process of remodeling and not just focus on the completed job. As you make positive changes in your home, you will bring positive changes to your home environment, whether the project is adding a window or adding a room.

# WORKING WITH PROFESSIONALS

As mentioned in Chapter 1, you need information about the skills, abilities, and responsibilities of various professionals before you decide who should help with your project.

The *general building contractor* can handle all aspects of a remodeling or new construction project. Often a carpenter by trade, the contractor may actually do the work or divide it among subcontractors.

The *subcontractor* is also a contractor, but one who specializes in a particular trade. For example, the plumber, electrician, and roofing specialist are all subcontractors.

The general contractor has the nuts-and-bolts experience to see any job to completion. That means responsibility for getting the work done properly—on time, with high-quality workmanship, and in accordance with local codes. Specific responsibilities of the general contractor include:

■ Hiring the necessary work crew and subcontractors and assuming liability for the workers' safety and compensation insurance
■ Arranging for building permits and for on-site inspections
■ Selecting and scheduling delivery of building materials
■ Offering limited design assistance and advice on what's possible in the way of materials and what's practical in time and procedures.

The *architect* who specializes in remodeling and renovation can offer you three important services.

■ *Design services.* After discussing your remodeling goals and needs, the architect will create several concept plans for you to consider. He or she will show you sketches and floor plans to help you visualize the ideas and will revise these plans until you find a solution that satisfies your particular requirements. The architect will also help you to estimate costs and to make the design financially feasible.

■ *Working plans and specifications.* Once the design is finalized, the architect can produce a set of finished plans and specifications for you to submit to the building department, contractors, and subcontractors.

■ *Supervision.* If you choose, the architect will supervise your entire project, including suggesting various contractors, sending the plans out for bids, and inspecting the progress of the work on a regular basis.

Some architects belong to a professional association, the American Institute of Architects. Membership in the AIA is voluntary, however, and its lack is not a reflection of an architect's competence.

Other types of professionals offer many of the same services as an architect. You may hire them for design, working drawings, supervision, or all three. The method of payment, either by fee or on an hourly basis, is also similar.

The *building designer* offers general design skills much like those of the architect. The major difference is a matter of schooling and credentials, although the state may impose limits as to the extent of projects a building designer can do. The building designer may be licensed as a designer and have undergone formal training; or he or she may simply have exprience in the building trades. Membership in the American Institute of Building Designers is signified by the letters AIBD.

The *kitchen designer* is a specialist in the design of new and remodeled kitchens. The initials CKD tell you that the designer is a Certified Kitchen Designer, licensed and accredited by the American Institute of Kitchen Dealers.

The *draftsman* has the training and ability to take rough sketches of your ideas and draw up a complete set of working plans and specifications. He or she may offer limited design services, although these are primarily technical and not conceptual. The draftsman does not inspect or oversee construction and may be paid by the hour or a set fee.

The *interior designer* specializes in planning and furnishing interiors. His or her responsibilities include space planning and room layout, as well as the selection of furnishings and finishes such as carpeting, wall coverings, and color coordination. The initials ASID indicate that the designer belongs to the American Society of Interior Designers.

## Specifications and Materials

A complete list of specifications is an essential part of your working plan. This list specifies the exact size and quality of all materials to be used in your project. The specifications also cover various construction methods to be used and anything else not easily indicated on the drawings.

Complete specifications are critical if your remodeling is to be done by a contractor or subcontractors. They need the specs to bid on your project. If your specifications are inexact, assumptions will be made to fill in the gaps. As a result you won't be able to compare one bid with another.

Incomplete specifications can also mean trouble once construction begins. Anything not included on the list becomes an extra that can be painfully expensive. The best way to guarantee you'll get what you want is to put everything in writing. Your specifications then become a part of the written contract. As construction proceeds, you should inspect for follow-through.

A professional designer can draw up your plans and provide the specifications, based on your guidelines. If you draw your own plans, you must provide the specs yourself. This may take some time, but shouldn't be difficult if you've researched the products you want to include. You are able to say, for example, that you want french doors in your addition; in fact, you want a particular size and model number available from a specific manufacturer. This information goes down on your list of specifications.

In some instances your specifications will indicate only the type and quality of material, leaving the choice of a particular manufacturer to the contractor. For example, you may specify fiberglass insulation with an R-11 factor and interior walls clad with top-grade 1/2-inch wallboard. Your architect or contractor can select the specific brand names based on experience and local availability.

However, don't leave the important product choices to others. You should research available options for everything that's visible, such as plumbing fixtures, cabinets, floor coverings, light fixtures, and so forth. This is your project and your home.

While specifications indicate the quality and brand name of products, a materials list indicates the quantity of materials. If professionals are doing your remodeling, they will take care of this. But if you plan to do the work yourself, you'll need to develop your own list so you can compare the cost of materials from various suppliers. Go over your plans inch by inch and determine the size and quantity of each material. If your project is large, you may be able to take your plans to a building supplier or lumber yard and ask them to provide an itemized list of material costs.

Most lumber is now S4S—planed smooth on all four sides. Today the actual size of a 2 by 4 is $1\frac{1}{2}$ by $3\frac{1}{2}$ inches, and a 2-by-8 piece of lumber measures $1\frac{1}{2}$ by $7\frac{1}{4}$ inches.

### Getting Written Bids

Once you have a working plan with specifications, you can get firm bids on your project; or your designer may handle this for you. You should plan to get at least three written bids for any job. But use your judgment here. If yours is a major remodeling, you may want to talk with six or more different contractors. The process of getting bids costs you nothing except your time. The more bids you have, the better you'll be able to evaluate what the job should really cost. If you are acting as your own general contractor, you'll need to get bids from as many different subcontractors as your plans require.

Be sure to provide each contractor with identical plans and specifications. This is the only way to compare their figures. If you add or change items, notify each bidder in writing. Depending on the complexity of your project, and how busy a contractor is, getting a written bid may take a week or more.

After you have the bids in hand, beware of any that are exceptionally low. Perhaps the contractor made a mistake or overlooked part of the work to be done. Unfortu-nately, some contractors bid too low just to get the job and once they begin to lose money simply walk away from the job. Your only recourse then is legal action.

On some jobs you may be better off working with a contractor on a time-and-materials or cost-plus basis. The quality of the work may be better with this arrangement. The contractor won't be rushing through your project because of an initial low bid. However, fixed price or maximum price arrangements are usually preferable.

If you have the time to help out during the work, you may be able to save money. For example, you can save the contractor's time by picking up supplies or materials as needed. Talk to the contractor about this. And shop around. You may decide you're better off with a skilled carpenter working on a cost-plus basis rather than a remodeling contractor working with a firm bid. Be sure to check personal referrals before you agree to any cost-plus arrangement.

### Working Out a Contract

Once you've selected a contractor or subcontractor, you're ready to work out a contract. An essential part of any contract is the method of payment. This can vary, depending on what you negotiate with the contractor. Also, the terms of your loan may stipulate how payment is to be made.

It's important to make sure the payment schedule is based on the contractor's performance. Generally, you should negotiate terms that require you to pay only for work that has been done. For example, you may agree to make payments as specified sections of the job are completed. Or the payments can be based on progress billing, which means the contractor will submit a monthly invoice for work that's been done.

Whatever the payment schedule, be sure to negotiate a retention clause in your contract. This means a certain percentage of the cost of the job, perhaps 10 percent, is to be withheld until the job is completed satisfactorily. Some contractors may require a deposit in advance as an indication of good faith. If so, find out if your state sets limitations on the size of the deposit, and how it's to be paid.

A contract should be precisely written, with no room for ambiguity. If you have any doubts, have an attorney look it over before you sign. The contract should include:

■ A detailed description of the work to be done by the contractor, as well as any work you've agreed to do yourself. Include specific provisions for clearing the site of debris during and after the project.

■ The type and grade of materials to be used for the job. These and possible substitutions may be covered in your list of specifications attached to the project.

■ The total cost of the work, with a schedule of payments and the amount of each payment.

■ Provisions for payment holdbacks, including a retention clause.

■ The approximate dates when the work will begin and when it will be completed. Include a completion clause penalty if these dates are not met.

■ A close-out clause so that you or the contractor may terminate the agreement if things begin to go sour. You may also want to include a provision for arbitration in the event of a dispute.

■ Provisions for the removal of property liens. If the contractor goes bankrupt or fails to pay any subcontractors or suppliers, they can file a lien against your property. And if that happens, you could lose your home or end up paying twice for the same work. This clause protects you by making the contractor responsible for obtaining property lien releases from subcontractors and suppliers as the work progresses.

You can also protect yourself by asking the contractor to secure a payment and completion bond. If the contractor fails to complete the job as specified, or doesn't pay the subcontractors or suppliers, the bond provides the money you need to finish your project. The bonding fee is usually 1 to 5 percent of the contract price.

# INDEX